P9-CKD-813

TEACHING AND USING DOCUMENT-BASED QUESTIONS FOR MIDDLE SCHOOL

EDWARD O'CONNOR

TEACHER IDEAS PRESS
PORTSMOUTH, NH

WITHDRAWN

TO PATTY—WITH ALL MY LOVE.

Teacher Ideas Press
A division of Reed Elsevier Inc.
361 Hanover Street
Portsmouth, NH 0380-3912
www.teacherideaspress.com

Offices and agents throughout the world

© 2004 by Edward O'Connor

All rights reserved. No part of this book may be reproduced in any form or by any
electronic or mechanical means, including information storage and retrieval systems,
without permission in writing from the publisher, except by a reviewer, who may quote
brief passages in a review. Reproducible pages may be copied for classroom and
educational programs with the exception of the excerpt, "I, Too, Sing America,"
from *The Collected Poems of Langston Hughes* by Langston Hughes, located on page 110.

The author and publisher wish to thank those who have generously given permission to reprint borrowed material.
A list of permissions can be found on page 194.

Library of Congress Cataloging-in Publication Data

O'Connor, Edward P.
    Teaching and using document-based questions for middle school / Edward P. O'Connor.
        p. cm.
    ISBN 1-56308-974-2
    1. United States—History—Study and teaching (Middle school) 2. United States—History—Sources. I. Title.

    E175.8 .O27 2003
    973'.071'2—dc22   2003014229

Editor: Suzanne Barchers
Production Coordinator: Angela Laughlin
Typesetter: Westchester Book Services
Cover design: Joni Doherty
Manufacturing: Steve Bernier

Printed in the United States of America on acid-free paper

08   07   06   05   04   VP   1   2   3   4   5

CONTENTS

ACKNOWLEDGMENTS V

INTRODUCTION VII

  1. Native American Cultures 1

  2. The Age of Exploration 9

  3. Democracy in Colonial America 19

  4. Loyalists and Patriots in the Revolution 27

  5. Political Parties and the New Nation 37

  6. Differences Between the North and the South 47

  7. Slavery in the United States 58

  8. Reconstruction 69

  9. Immigration 79

10. The Growth of Industry 90

11. The Progressive Era 99

12. America in the 1920s 108

13. The Great Depression and the New Deal 119

14. America in World War II 129

15. America and the Cold War 140

16. The Civil Rights Movement 151

APPENDIX I: RUBRIC FOR SCAFFOLDING QUESTIONS 161

APPENDIX II: INTERNET RESOURCES 181

SOURCES FOR WORKS CITED 185

COPYRIGHT ACKNOWLEDGMENTS 194

INDEX 195

ABOUT THE AUTHOR 197

ACKNOWLEDGMENTS

I would like to extend grateful acknowledgment to the many people who lent assistance to the production of this book. My thanks to those who helped me obtain photographs and other visual documents for the activities: Coi Gehrig of the Denver Public Library, Dana Kanabrocki of the Gilder Lehrman Collection, Stephanie Jacobe of the Virginia Historical Society, Tom Lisante and the staff of the New York Public Library, and Kathy Hubenschmidt of the Arizona State Museum, as well as the staffs of both the National Archives and the Library of Congress.

I am grateful to my colleagues at Arlington Middle School in Poughkeepsie, NY: Andy Arenson, Laurie Brown, Rick Butler, Christa Connors, Mike Tucci, Dan Sims, and Ernie Verdis. They provided me with invaluable support, advice, feedback, and suggestions, and are a unique collection of dedicated, enthusiastic teachers. I am fortunate to work with and learn from them.

I owe a great deal of thanks to my parents, Jim and Therese O'Connor. There is no end to the love and support they extend to their children.

Working on this book over the course of a year took a great deal of my time and attention, as well as much patience and understanding on the part of my children, Maeve and Liam. My wife, Patty, besides doing far more than her fair share at home, offered sound advice and valuable opinions, and was generally the objective and clear voice of reason throughout a very busy year.

INTRODUCTION

The purpose of this book is to give teachers the opportunity to challenge students to analyze documents, think critically, and draw conclusions based on evidence. Essentially, Document-Based Questions (DBQs) offer students the opportunity to think and act like historians. Instead of having issues in American History explained to them students can explore them in thoughtful and meaningful ways.

DBQs have long been featured on Advanced Placement tests put out by the Educational Testing Service. In 2001, New York State made them a part of their testing program, utilizing DBQs in their fifth- and eighth-grade Assessments, as well as the tenth- and eleventh-grade Regents exams.

In addition to their use in standardized testing, DBQs have been used as a means of assessing student progress in social studies, because these activities involve many of the skills stressed by teachers. Some of the skills that are involved in Document-Based Questions include: content area reading, reading graphs, charts, and tables, interpretation of visuals such as drawings and photographs, and most of all, expository writing.

Each chapter in this book consists of two parts. **Part A**, the "scaffolding," involves between six and nine documents with short-answer questions that go along with each document. Most textual documents have been slightly edited to accommodate younger readers, but some passages can be challenging. Students will carefully examine each document and respond to the questions that follow. The point value for each question is in parentheses at the end of the space provided for answers, and rubrics for scoring answers are in Appendix I.

Part B is the essay portion of the DBQ in which students address all parts of the task in a well-organized and well-written essay that specifically refers to more than half of the documents. (E.g.: If there are nine documents, students are to utilize at least five of them.) For full credit, students may also include information beyond what is provided in the unit's documents. A rubric for evaluating the essay accompanies each chapter.

Teachers should prepare packets for student use by photocopying the cover page of each unit (Directions and Historical Context) and the entire short-answer section. The essay question/evaluation form can also be included in this packet, or teachers can give it to students separately, later on, as they see fit.

When assigning a DBQ unit, teachers should direct students' attention to the task listed on the first page of that unit. The task lists the topics that students will later address in their essays, and they should keep them in mind as they complete the short-answer section because they will refer to these topics as documents when writing their essays.

This book covers sixteen major themes of study in American history, from Native American Culture to the Civil Rights movement. Teachers will find these activities useful in assessing students' skill and knowledge, as review activities, or, in some cases, as a teaching tool in support of the unit itself. DBQs can be difficult, but students learn best when challenged with meaningful activities.

1

⚜

DBQ THEME:
NATIVE AMERICAN CULTURES

DIRECTIONS:

This task is based on the accompanying documents (1–6). Some of these documents have been edited to help you with the task. The essay is designed to test your ability to work with historical documents and your knowledge of Native American cultures. Carefully analyze the documents as you complete **Part A**. Your responses should help you to write the essay in **Part B**.

HISTORICAL CONTEXT:

For thousands of years, Native American tribes developed and flourished throughout North and South America. These cultures developed very differently from one another, largely due to the various climates and lands to which they had to adapt. To survive in sometimes harsh environments, Native Americans had to put a great deal of time and energy into making the most of the natural resources that were available to them.

TASK:

- Describe at least three natural environments Native Americans adapted to in North America.
- Discuss specific steps Native Americans took to survive in these environments.

PART A—SHORT-ANSWER SECTION

The following documents relate to Native American cultures. Examine each document carefully and answer the questions that follow it.

Document 1: Native American Culture Chart

TRIBE	GEOGRAPHIC LOCATION	TYPE OF CLIMATE	LIFESTYLE	FOOD	SHELTER
IROQUOIS	Eastern Woodlands; Upstate New York	Humid Continental-Four seasons: cold winter, hot summer and mild in spring and fall	Permanent villages surrounded by palisades (high wall made of wood) for protection.	Agriculture-corn beans and squash. Hunted deer, deer, bear, fish and other game	Longhouse-made of saplings and tree bark.
INUIT	Northern Alaska, Canada and Greenland	Arctic-very cold throughout the year.	Small bands; on the move frequently in search of food	Hunted seals, fish, whales walruses and caribou.	Homes made of wood, sod, stone and animal skin. Igloos made of snow served as temporary shelter in winter.
SIOUX	Western Great Plains	Steppe-Hot dry summers, cold winters	Villages were mobile. Tipis and other belongings could be packed up and moved on travois.	Hunted bufalo and other game Gathered wild plants, nuts and berries.	Tipi – made of buffalo skin and supported by wooden poles
HOPI	Southwestern United States	Desert and Steppe	Permanent villages near rivers that could be used to irrigate crops	Agriculture-corn beans and squash. Raised turkeys. Hunted for game.	Large buildings several stories high made of adobe (mud brick) and rock.

1. Name two Native American groups that did not develop agriculture.

_____(2)

2. Give two examples of how the Inuit were affected by living in an arctic climate.

_____

_____(2)

May be copied for classroom use. *Teaching and Using Document-Based Questions for Middle School* by Edward O'Connor (Portsmouth, NH: Teacher Ideas Press); ©2004.

Document 2: Hohokum Irrigation Canals

Courtesy Arizona State Museum, University of Arizona

This is a photo of canals built by the Hohokum and unearthed by archaeologists at Snaketown, Arizona. The Hohokum constructed hundreds of miles of canals throughout the dry lands of the southwest.

1. What are two things for which the Hohokum used these canals?

_____

_____(2)

2. Why would the Hohokum need to build canals like this to survive?

_____

_____

_____(1)

Document 3: Making Canoes in Virginia (1722)

When in their travels, if the Indians meet with any waters that cannot be crossed, they make canoes of birch bark, by slipping it whole off the tree, in this manner. First, they gash the bark quite round the tree, at the length they would want the canoe to be, then slit down the length from end to end; when that is done, they with their tomahawks easily open up the bark, and strip it whole off. Then they force it open with sticks in the middle, slope the underside with the ends, and sow them up, which helps keep the belly open; or if the birch trees happen to be small, they sow the bark of two together. The seams they coat with clay or mud, and then pass over the water in their canoes, by two, three or more at a time, according to their size. By reason of the lightness of these boats, they can easily carry them over land, if they foresee that they are likely to meet with any more waters that may get in their way . . .

1. What is the advantage of making canoes that are light?

_____

_____

_____

_____(1)

2. Name at least two materials found in nature used to make a canoe.

_____

_____

_____

_____(2)

Document 4: Description of a Native American Home (Kansas 1869)

. . . it seemed as though the level plain was dotted with huge hay stacks . . . but how symmetrical and beautiful: thirty to forty feet high, and as though they were laid out by the rules of geometry! As we near them we soon discover that our hay stacks are the houses of the Witchitas, built of straw, thatched layer upon layer, with stout bindings of willow-saplings, tied together with buffalo hide or stripped hickory. They invite you in with much politeness, and, accepting their hospitality, you find yourself in a clean and comfortable dwelling.

In the center is the fire. Around the sides the beds are fitted up on bunks raised three feet from the floor, built of split-boards, tied together with cords made of buffalo hide. The floor is hard packed earth, clean as can be. The builders have wisely made the best of their resources. The grass, willow-saplings, buffalo hide etc. . . . are all found close at hand; and out of these, which would not have been any use to us in house-building, the Witchitas have built the most convenient homes.

1. What are two ways that the Witchitas used buffalo hide, according to this passage?

_____

_____

_____

_____(2)

2. According to the author, how have the Witchitas made good use of their natural resources?

_____

_____

_____

_____(2)

Document 5: Photograph of Cheyenne Tipis and Travois

Courtesy Denver Public Library

Many Plains tribes would join two poles with a frame to create a travois, like the one shown above. Pulled by a horse, the travois enabled people to move their tipis and other belongings easily as they pursued buffalo herds.

1. For what did Native Americans on the Great Plains use the travois?

_____

_____

_____

_____

_____(1)

2. Why would hunters like the Cheyenne shown here need to be able to move their belongings?

_____

_____

_____

_____

_____(1)

Document 6: An Indian Boy's Training

It seems to be a popular idea that all Indians are born with the skills and instincts for which they are well known. This is a mistake. All the patience and skills of the Indian are acquired traits, and continual practice alone makes him the master of the art of wood-craft. My uncle, who educated me up to the age of fifteen years, was a strict disciplinarian, and a good teacher. When I left the tipi in the morning, he would say, "Hakadah, look closely at everything you see"; and at evening, on my return he would often instruct me for an hour or so. . . . He meant to make me observant and a good student of nature.

"Hakadah," he would say to me, "it is better to view animals unobserved. I have been witness to many of their courtships and quarrels and have learned many of their secrets in this way . . . I advise you, never to approach a grizzly's den from the front, but to steal up behind and throw your blanket or a stone in front of the hole. He does not usually rush for it, but first puts his head out and listens and then comes out very slowly . . . While he is exposing himself in this fashion, aim at his heart. Always be as cool as the animal himself." This is how he armed me against the cunning of the savage beasts, by teaching me how to outwit them.

1. What are two things the author was taught by his uncle?

_____

_____

_____

_____

_____(2)

2. According to this passage, what are two traits that Indians must develop to be masters of wood-

craft? _____

_____

_____

_____

_____(2)

PART B—ESSAY: NATIVE AMERICAN CULTURES

TASK:

Using the documents in your packet, your answers to the questions in Part A, and your knowledge of social studies, write a well-developed essay that includes an introduction, supporting paragraphs, and a conclusion in which you thoroughly address the following:

- Describe at least three natural environments that Native Americans adapted to in North America.
- Discuss specific steps Native Americans took to survive in these environments.

NOTE: *your essay will be evaluated using the form below.*

	Point Value	Points Earned
Effective use of documents— *uses at least 4 documents*	15	_____
Accuracy— *includes correct information*	15	_____
Depth and detail— *supports main ideas with facts*	10	_____
Knowledge of social studies— *uses information beyond supplied documents*	10	_____
Clarity/Organization— *clearly expresses and logically develops ideas*	10	_____
Language mechanics— *uses proper spelling, grammar, and style*	10	_____
Correct format— *includes introduction, supporting paragraphs, and conclusion*	10	_____
TOTAL	**80**	_____

Comments: _____

_____

_____

Part A Score _____   Part B Score _____   **TOTAL SCORE** _____

2

DBQ THEME:
THE AGE OF EXPLORATION

DIRECTIONS:

This task is based on the accompanying documents (1–8). Some of these documents have been edited to help you with the task. The essay is designed to test your ability to work with historical documents and your knowledge of the Age of Exploration. Carefully analyze the documents as you complete **Part A**. Your responses should help you to write the essay in **Part B**.

HISTORICAL CONTEXT:

The Age of Exploration (1400–1700) had a tremendous impact on the history of the world. Before this, there had been no lasting contact between the New World (the Americas) and the Old World (Europe, Africa, and Asia). Beginning with the Portuguese in the mid-1400s, European explorers went on voyages of discovery, in search of riches and glory. The places and people that they came in contact with, as well as the exploring nations themselves, were forever changed.

TASK:

- Identify and discuss at least three factors that led to the Age of Exploration.
- Identify and discuss at least three effects of the Age of Exploration.

PART A—SHORT-ANSWER SECTION

The following documents relate to the Age of Exploration. Examine each document carefully and answer the questions that follow.

Document 1: Description of Beijing, China by Marco Polo (1271)

> *The city is the business center of the world. All the most precious stones and pearls from India are brought there. The strangest and most valuable things come from Cathay and other nearby provinces. All these rare items reach Beijing because the court is there with all its fine ladies, noblemen, soldiers and others who attend to the Emperor, Kublai Kahn. At least 1,000 cartloads of silk are sent to Beijing every day. Vast quantities of silk and cloth of gold are woven there because there is a scarcity of flax and cotton. There are more than 200 cities in the surrounding area from which people come to Beijing to buy and sell produce, which is why the city is such an important trading center.*

1. According to the author, why is Beijing such an important trading center?

_____

_____

_____

_____

_____(1)

2. What items were sold in Beijing that Europeans would want?

_____

_____

_____

_____

_____(2)

May be copied for classroom use. *Teaching and Using Document-Based Questions for Middle School* by Edward O'Connor (Portsmouth, NH: Teacher Ideas Press); ©2004.

Document 2: The Caravel

Courtesy Print Collection, New York Public Library

Many European explorers used caravels, which had triangular (lateen) sails and a rudder for steering. These features helped make long ocean voyages possible.

1. Name a feature of the caravel that made long-distance voyages possible.

_____

_____

_____(1)

Document 3: Hernan Cortes Calls for Volunteers (1519)

It was proclaimed by beat of drum and sound of trumpet, that all those that entered the service of the expedition against the Aztecs should have their share of what gold was obtained, and grants of land as soon as the conquest was completed. The proclamation was no sooner made, than volunteers offered themselves everywhere. Nothing was to be seen or heard but of purchasing weapons and horses, making coats of armor, and preparing bread and salting pork for the expedition.

1. What are two things soldiers expected to gain from joining Cortes in his expedition against the

Aztecs? _____

_____

_____

_____(2)

2. Name at least two items the soldiers prepared to bring with them on this journey that could be used

in battle against the Aztecs. _____

_____

_____(2)

Document 4: The Astrolabe

Courtesy the Adler Planetarium and Astronomy Museum, Chicago IL

Explorers found the astrolabe to be an extremely valuable instrument. Using certain stars or the noon-time sun, sailors could use the astrolabe to locate their latitude.

1. Why was the astrolabe valuable to European explorers?

_____

_____

_____

_____

_____(1)

Document 5: Excerpt from *A Brief Account of the Devastation of the Indies,* **by Bartolome de las Casas (1548)**

> . . . *of all the infinite universe of humanity, the Indians are the most sincere, they do not possess any wickedness or deceitfulness at all. They are by nature the most humble, patient and peaceable people; they hold no grudges and are neither overly emotional nor argumentative. And because they are so meek and eager to please, they are less able to endure heavy labor and soon die. . . .*
>
> *And into this herd of sheep, into this land of meek outcasts, there came some Spaniards who immediately behaved like wild beasts: wolves, tigers, or lions that had been starved for many days. And Spaniards have behaved in no other way during the last forty years, to the present time, for they are still acting like savage beasts, killing, terrorizing, torturing and destroying the native peoples, doing all this with the strangest and most varied new methods of cruelty, never seen or heard of before, and to such a degree that this island of Hispanola, once so populous (over three million), has now a population of barely two hundred persons.*
>
> *The island of Cuba is now almost completely depopulated. Puerto Rico and Jamaica are two of the largest, most productive and attractive islands; both are now deserted and devastated. The Bahamas have the healthiest lands in the world, where lived more than five hundred thousand souls; they are now deserted, inhabited by not a single living creature. All the people were slain or died after being taken into captivity and brought to the Island of Hispanola to be sold as slaves.*
>
> *All in all, we can estimate very surely and truthfully that in the forty years that the Spanish have been involved in the New World, with the infernal actions of the Spanish Christians, there have been unjustly slain more than twelve million men, women, and children. In truth, I believe without trying to deceive myself that the number of the slain is more like fifteen million.*

1. Name two reasons why there were no people living in the Bahamas, according to de las Casas.

_____

_____(2)

2. According to the author, how many Native Americans were killed by the Spanish?

_____

_____(1)

Document 6: A Slave Factory in Africa

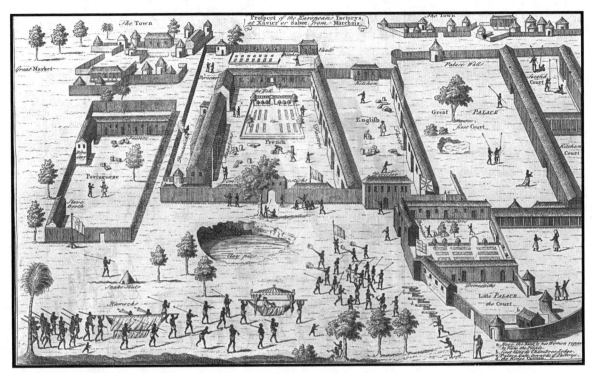

Courtesy Library of Congress

This is a drawing of a European fortress in what is now Nigeria, on the coast of West Africa. Compounds like these were important to slave traders, and were often called "slave factories." After capture, slaves were brought to the fortress and forced to wait for long periods of time in dark, damp dungeons before being boarded onto slave ships bound for the New World.

1. Why was this fortress built on the coast?

_____

_____

_____

_____(1)

Document 7: An Argument for Colonization—Richard Hakluyt (1584)

Starting colonies in North America may prevent the Spanish king from flowing all over North America; if we do it quickly, we can prevent him from making use of the ports in the lands we have claimed. . . . And when England possesses these lands her Majesty [Queen Elizabeth I] may have plenty of excellent trees for masts of good timber to build ships and make great navies . . . and all for no price, and without money or having to ask. How easy a matter it may be to this country, having the best and smartest shipwrights of the world to be lords of the seas, and to spoil the Spanish navy, and to deprive them of free and easy passage of their treasure into Europe and consequently to reduce the pride of Spain . . .

1. According to Hakluyt, what should England do with lumber from the New World?

    _____

    _____

    _____

    _____

    _____(1)

2. Name two ways that England could limit Spanish power in the New World, according to Hakluyt.

    _____

    _____

    _____

    _____(2)

Document 8: The Columbian Exchange

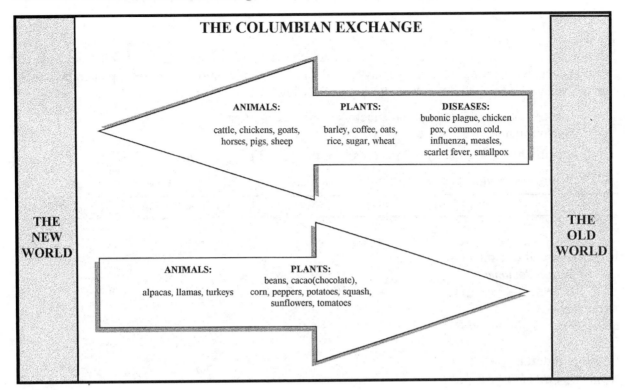

When Europeans explored the New World, they found many types of plants and animals that were previously unknown to the Old World. Likewise, many types of plants and animals, as well as European diseases, were introduced into the Americas. This migration is known as the Columbian Exchange, and is represented by the chart above.

1. What are some important plants that Europeans encountered in the New World?

_____

_____

_____(2)

2. Name at least two diseases Europeans brought to the New World.

_____

_____

_____(2)

NAME _____ DATE _____

PART B—ESSAY: THE AGE OF EXPLORATION

TASK:

Using the documents in your packet, your answers to the questions in Part A, and your knowledge of social studies, write a well-developed essay that includes an introduction, supporting paragraphs, and a conclusion in which you thoroughly address the following:

- Identify and discuss at least three factors that led to the Age of Exploration.
- Identify and discuss at least three effects of the Age of Exploration.

NOTE: *your essay will be evaluated using the form below.*

	Point Value	Points Earned
Effective use of documents— *uses at least 5 documents*	15	_____
Accuracy— *includes correct information*	15	_____
Depth and detail— *supports main ideas with facts*	10	_____
Knowledge of social studies— *uses information beyond supplied documents*	10	_____
Clarity/Organization— *clearly expresses and logically develops ideas*	10	_____
Language mechanics— *uses proper spelling, grammar, and style*	10	_____
Correct format— *includes introduction, supporting paragraphs, and conclusion*	10	_____
TOTAL	**80**	_____

Comments: _____

_____

_____

Part A Score _____   Part B Score _____   **TOTAL SCORE** _____

3

DBQ THEME:
DEMOCRACY IN COLONIAL AMERICA

DIRECTIONS:

This task is based on the accompanying documents (1–6). Some of these documents have been edited to help you with the task. The essay is designed to test your ability to work with historical documents and your knowledge of colonial America. Carefully analyze the documents as you complete **Part A**. Your responses should help you to write the essay in **Part B**.

HISTORICAL CONTEXT:

Due to British political traditions, distance from the mother country, and other factors, the thirteen colonies in America began early on to develop democratic features. Despite this, many aspects of colonial life were strikingly undemocratic. A close look at that time period suggests that colonial democracy was a work in progress.

TASK:

- Identify and discuss two democratic and two undemocratic features of colonial America.

- Explain how American democracy was a work in progress in colonial times.

PART A—SHORT-ANSWER SECTION

The following documents relate to colonial America. Examine each document carefully and answer the questions that follow it.

Document 1: Maryland's Act of Toleration (1649)

> *. . . because the enforcing of the conscience in matters of religion has frequently shown to be of dangerous consequence in those colonies where it has been practiced, and for the more quiet and peaceful government of this province, and the better to preserve mutual love and friendship amongst the inhabitants of the colony; be it therefore with the advice and consent of this assembly ordered and enacted . . . that no person or persons within Maryland professing to believe in any form of Christianity shall from now on be in any way troubled, interfered with or embarrassed in respect to his or her religion, nor in the free exercise thereof . . .*

1. According to this document, why did the Assembly of Maryland create this law?

_____

_____

_____

_____(1)

2. What freedom is protected by this law?

_____

_____

_____

_____(1)

3. Name at least one specific group of people that would not be protected by this law.

_____

_____(1)

May be copied for classroom use. *Teaching and Using Document-Based Questions for Middle School* by Edward O'Connor (Portsmouth, NH: Teacher Ideas Press); ©2004.

DEMOCRACY IN COLONIAL AMERICA

Document 2: Voting Qualifications (1763)

COLONY	RELIGION	RACE	GENDER	PROPERTY
NEW HAMPSHIRE	Christian	White	Male	Land valued at £ 50 *
MASSACHUSETTS	Christian	White	Male	Land rented at £2 /year or total possessions £40
RHODE ISLAND	Christian	White	Male	Land rented at £2/year or total possessions £40
CONNECTICUT	Christian	White	Male	Land rented at £2/year or total possessions £40
NEW YORK	Christian	White	Male	Land valued at £ 40
NEW JERSEY	Christian	White	Male	Land valued at £ 50 *
PENNSYLVANIA	Christian	White	Male	50 Acres or land valued at £ 50
DELAWARE	Christian	White	Male	50 Acres or land valued at £ 40
MARYLAND	Christian	White	Male	50 Acres or land valued at £ 40
VIRGINIA	Christian	White	Male	25 Acres with a house or 100 acres without
NORTH CAROLINA	Christian	White	Male	50 Acres *
SOUTH CAROLINA	Christian	White	Male	50 Acres or land rented at £2/year *
GEORGIA	Christian	White	Male	50 Acres *

* Property requirements in these colonies were higher for candidates for office.

£1 in 1763 equals approximately $132 in the year 2000. Source: Purvis, Thomas L. Colonial America to 1763.

1. Name at least two of the main requirements for voting in the thirteen colonies.

_____

_____

_____(2)

2. Name at least two groups of people that could not vote in colonial America.

_____

_____

_____(2)

Document 3: The Fundamental Orders of Connecticut (1639)

"... It is ordered that there be yearly two General Assemblies or Courts ... and a governor shall be chosen for the year and shall have power to administer justice according to the laws here established. The choice for governor shall be made by all those who are eligible to vote ...

"It is ordered that no person be chosen governor more than once in two years ...

"It is ordered that every General Court shall include the governor, to moderate the court ... and if the governor neglects or refuses to call the General Court into session, the voters may do so. ... In the General Court shall rest supreme power of the colony, and they only shall have power to make laws or repeal them, to levy taxes, dispose of unclaimed land; they shall have the power to call public officials or any other person into question for any misdemeanor and may with good reason remove or deal otherwise accordingly with the offender ..."

1. Name at least two powers given to the General Court in this document.

_____

_____

_____(2)

2. Describe at least two democratic features of Connecticut's government.

_____

_____

_____(2)

3. Name two ways that the power of Connecticut's governor was limited by this document.

_____

_____

_____(2)

Document 4: Title Page from *The Lady's Law* (first published 1733)

Courtesy Virginia Historical Society

This document is the title page of a book that included many of the legal restrictions faced by *"femme coverts,"* women legally dependent on a husband. Once married, colonial women could not own property or collect wages. Men routinely gained custody of children in cases of divorce.

Note: in colonial-era texts, a lower case 's' often looks like a lower case 'f'. To help today's students interpret this old style, chapter headings have been reprinted below.

I. Of Descents of Lands to Females, Coparceners, etc. . .

II. Of Consummation of Marriage, Stealing of Women, Rapes, Polygamy.

III. Of the Laws of Procreation of Children, and of Illegitimate Children.

IV. Of the Privileges of Femme Coverts, and Their Power in Regard to Their Husbands, and all Others.

V. Of Husband and Wife, in what Actions they are to Join.

VI. Of the Limitations on Inheritance of Estates, Jointures and Settlements, Real and Personal of Women.

VII. Of What the Wife is Entitled To of the Husband's, and things Belonging to the Wife, the Husband gains Possession of in Marriage.

VIII. Of Private Contracts by the Wife, Alimony, Separate Maintenance, Divorces, Elopement, etc. . .

1. What happened to property a woman owned if she got married?

_____

_____(1)

2. According to this document, how were women unequal to men in colonial times?

_____

_____(1)

Document 5: Plan of a Slave Ship

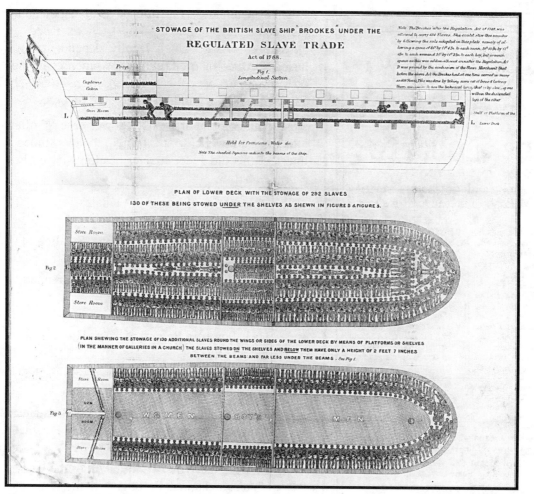

Courtesy Library of Congress

Although slavery existed in all thirteen colonies, it quickly became a vital part of the southern economy. Slavery was a permanent, hereditary condition. Slaves had no legal rights and were forbidden to read or write. The document above suggests the horrible conditions on board a slave ship.

1. Describe two ways in which slave traders were able to fit a large number of slaves onto their ships.

_____

_____(2)

2. Name at least one undemocratic feature of the colonies that is shown in this document.

_____

_____(1)

Document 6: Engraving of Virginia's House of Burgesses

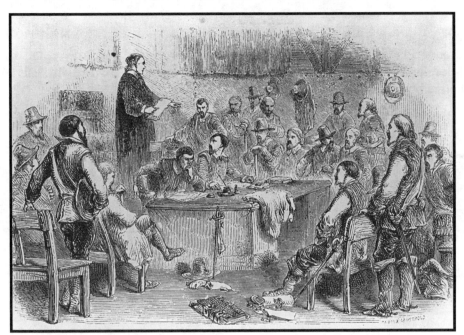

Courtesy Library of Congress

This engraving depicts the first meeting of Virginia's House of Burgesses in 1619. This legislature was made up of representatives chosen by popular vote. Eventually, every colony in America would have such a legislature.

1. What activity or activities are depicted here that suggest the importance of a legislature?

_____

_____

_____

_____(1)

2. How did the House of Burgesses allow citizens to have a voice in government?

_____

_____

_____

_____(1)

NAME _____ DATE _____

PART B—ESSAY: DEMOCRACY IN COLONIAL AMERICA

TASK:

Using the documents in your packet, your answers to the questions in Part A, and your knowledge of social studies, write a well-developed essay that includes an introduction, supporting paragraphs, and a conclusion in which you thoroughly address the following:

- Identify and discuss two democratic and two undemocratic features of colonial America.
- Explain how democracy in America was a work in progress in colonial times.

NOTE: *your essay will be evaluated using the form below.*

	Point Value	Points Earned
Effective use of documents— *uses at least **4** documents*	15	_____
Accuracy— *includes correct information*	15	_____
Depth and detail— *supports main ideas with facts*	10	_____
Knowledge of social studies— *uses information beyond supplied documents*	10	_____
Clarity/Organization— *clearly expresses and logically develops ideas*	10	_____
Language mechanics— *uses proper spelling, grammar, and style*	10	_____
Correct format— *includes introduction, supporting paragraphs, and conclusion*	10	_____
TOTAL	**80**	_____

Comments: _____

_____

_____

Part A Score _____   Part B Score _____   **TOTAL SCORE** _____

4

DBQ THEME: LOYALISTS AND PATRIOTS IN THE REVOLUTION

DIRECTIONS:

This task is based on the accompanying documents (1–9). Some of these documents have been edited to help you with the task. The essay is designed to test your ability to work with historical documents and your knowledge of the American Revolution. Carefully analyze the documents as you complete **Part A**. Your responses should help you to write the essay in **Part B**.

HISTORICAL CONTEXT:

When the Revolutionary War began in 1775, Americans were forced to decide which side of the struggle they would support. Loyalists, sometimes called Tories, supported the mother country, while Patriots supported the rebellion in hopes of gaining independence from Great Britain. For most people, this was not an easy decision to make. There were numerous factors that needed to be considered beyond the important questions of American liberty or loyalty to the king. People thought about whether they would benefit more from an American or a British victory. Some were worried about their safety and shifted their support between both sides, depending on who seemed to be winning.

TASK:

- Discuss at least two reasons why Americans would choose to be Loyalists and support Britain during the Revolutionary War.
- Discuss at least two reasons why Americans would choose to be Patriots and support American independence during the Revolutionary War.

PART A—SHORT-ANSWER SECTION

The following documents relate to the Revolutionary War. Examine each document carefully and answer the questions that follow.

Document 1: The Boston Massacre (1770)

© American Antiquarian Society

Tensions between Britain and her colonies had been growing steadily for several years when five Americans were shot and killed during a riot on March 5, 1770. Although it does not show events accurately, this famous engraving by Paul Revere helped to increase Americans' outrage over the Boston Massacre.

1. What are two ways that this picture makes the British look bad?

_____

_____(2)

May be copied for classroom use. *Teaching and Using Document-Based Questions for Middle School* by Edward O'Connor (Portsmouth, NH: Teacher Ideas Press); ©2004.

Document 2: A Loyalist is Tarred and Feathered (1774)

The most shocking cruelty occurred a few nights ago, upon a poor old man named Malcolm. A quarrel was picked with him, he was afterward taken and tarred and feathered. He was stripped stark naked, on one of the coldest nights this winter, his body covered all over with tar, then with feathers, his arm dislocated in tearing off his clothes. He was dragged in a cart with thousands taking part, some beating him with clubs and knocking him out of the cart, then in again. They gave him several severe whippings, at different parts of the town. Under torture, they demanded him to curse the King, Governor etc., which they could not make him do, but he still cried, "Curse all traitors!" The doctors say that it is impossible this poor creature can live. These events serve to show the hopeless state of government and the lawlessness and barbarism of the times. No person is safe.

1. Why was Malcolm treated in this way?

_____

_____(1)

2. How does the author show that she is a Loyalist?

_____

_____(1)

Document 3: The Continental Congress Explains the Need to Fight (1775)

The following passage is taken from a document that was written by John Dickinson of Pennsylvania and Thomas Jefferson of Virginia, and is known as the "Declaration of the Causes and Necessity of Taking Up Arms".

> *In brief, these colonies now feel the disasters of fire, sword and famine. We are reduced to the choices of unconditionally giving in to an unfair government, or resistance by force. Honor, justice and humanity forbid us to tamely surrender the freedom which we have received from our brave ancestors, and which future generations have a right to receive from us.*
>
> *Our cause is just. Our union is perfect. Our natural resources are great, and if necessary, we will easily be able to get foreign assistance. With strong hearts, we most solemnly declare that the arms we have been forced by our enemies to take on, we will in defiance of every danger, work for the preservation of our liberties; our minds made up to die free men rather than to live as slaves.*
>
> *In our own native land, in defense of the freedom that is our birthright, and which we always enjoyed until recently—for the protection of our property, which we received only by the honest hard work of our forefathers and ourselves, against all violence we have endured, we have taken up arms. We shall lay them down when the violence has ceased on the part of Britain, and not before.*

1. Name two reasons the Americans felt the need to take up arms against Britain.

_____

_____

_____

_____(2)

2. According to this document, what would be the result if Americans did not fight Britain?

_____

_____

_____

_____(1)

LOYALISTS AND PATRIOTS IN THE REVOLUTION

Document 4: A Comparison of Strength

A COMPARISON OF BRITISH AND AMERICAN MILITARY AND FINANCIAL POWER
1775–1783

COUNTRY	ARMY	NAVY	FINANCES
GREAT BRITAIN	* One of the best in the world. * Well trained and disciplined. * Well equipped. * Hired 30,000 Hessians (German mercenaries)	* Best in the world * 131 ships of the line (at least 64 guns each) * Hundreds of other ships	* British pound * Currency of stable value * Well established system of taxation and finance * Britain spent 4.5 million pounds on Hessians alone.
UNITED STATES	* Continental Army created in 1775 * Never more than 20,000 men at one time * Did not receive adequate formal training until winter 1777-1778 * Problems with pay and lack of supplies led to many mutinies and desertions	* Continental Navy created in 1775 * Never numbered more than 64 ships at any one time * Most ships were frigates (smaller than ships of the line)	* Continental Dollar established 1775 * Value of the dollar dropped throughout the war. * Dollar lost 90% of its value by 1779 * By 1781 only "hard money" (gold, silver) used in U.S. markets

1. How did British financial power help make their military strong?

_____

_____

_____

_____(1)

2. According to this chart, which side seemed more likely to win the Revolutionary War? Be sure to

explain your answer. _____

_____

_____

_____(2)

Document 5: A Description of the Continental Army (1775)

The army is not very badly equipped, but most wretchedly clothed, and as dirty a set of mortals as ever disgraced the name of a soldier. They have had no clothes of any sort provided for them by the Congress, though the army in general, and the Massachusetts forces in particular, had encouragement of having coats given them for enlisting. The neglect of the Congress to fulfill their promise in this respect has been the source of a great deal of uneasiness among the soldiers.

Another reason why the army can never be well united and regulated is the disagreement and jealousies between the different troops from the different colonies; which will never fail to create uneasiness among them. The Massachusetts forces already complain very loudly of the favor the General shows to the Virginians. The gentlemen of the Southern Colonies complain of the great number of New England officers in the army, and particularly those belonging to the colony of Massachusetts Bay.

Thus have these jealousies and uneasiness already begun, which I think cannot fail to increase and grow every day, and if they do not finally destroy the very existence of the army, they will certainly make it much less powerful than it otherwise might have been.

1. According to this account, what are two problems faced by the Continental Army?

_____

_____

_____

_____

_____(2)

2. How would these problems make it difficult for the Continental Army to be successful?

_____

_____

_____

_____

_____(1)

Document 6: An Excerpt from *Common Sense* by Thomas Paine (1776)

To the evils of monarchy, we must add that of hereditary succession—it is an insult to future generations, for no one by birth could have a right to set up his own family in power over all others forever; and although he himself might deserve some degree of honor, his descendants might be far too unworthy to inherit them . . . No man can have any other public honors than those that were given directly to him, so the givers of those honors have no power to give away the right of future generations by saying to a ruler, "your children and your children's children shall rule over ours forever." Such an unwise, unfair, and unnatural agreement might put the next generation under the government of a villain or a fool.

1. Explain why Thomas Paine calls monarchy an "unwise, unfair, and unnatural agreement."

_____

_____

_____

_____

_____(1)

Document 7: An excerpt from *Plain Truth* by James Chalmers (1776)

Can we suppose that Americans are capable of defending against the power of Great Britain? Our colonies, covered with navigable rivers, everywhere accessible to the fleets and armies of Britain, can make no defense. We must view our colonies, half armed, without money or a navy: We must confess that no people were ever opposed to such a powerful enemy while facing so many disadvantages . . . Can a reasonable person for a moment believe that Great Britain, whose political existence depends on our obedience, who but recently made such tremendous efforts to save us from France, will not exert herself as powerfully to save us from the wild schemes of independence?

1. Describe two of the arguments against American independence Chalmers gives in this passage.

_____

_____

_____

_____(2)

Document 8: Value of Trade with England 1763–1781

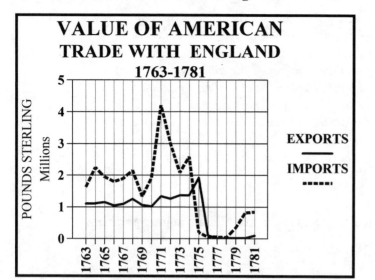

Source: American Historical Statistics

1. When were imports from England at their highest?

_____

_____

_____

_____

_____(1)

2. Overall, what effect did the Revolutionary War have on trade with England?

_____

_____

_____

_____(1)

Document 9: Song of the Minute Man (1777)

Come rise up brother Minute Men and let us have a chorus,
the braver and the bolder, the more they will adore us.
Our country calls for swords and musket balls, and drums aloud does rattle.
Our fifers charm "arise to arms", Liberty calls "to battle."

So let us not be dismayed although the Tories thunder,
They only want to ruin us and live upon our plunder.
Our cause is just and so we must with heaven's kind protection,
while [Lord] North and [General] Gage in all their rage will never come to action.

Now to our station let us march and rendezvous with pleasure,
we have been brave Minute Men to serve so great a treasure.
We let them see immediately that we are men of mettle,
we Jersey boys who fear no noise will never flinch from battle.

And when we do return again it will be with glory,
for them that do remain at home to hear a valiant story.
They will draw near and glad to hear no doubting of the wonder,
that Minute Men, though one to ten, should bring the Tories under.

1. According to this song, what were two reasons the Minute Men risked their lives?

_____

_____

_____

_____

_____(2)

PART B—ESSAY:
PATRIOTS AND LOYALISTS IN THE REVOLUTION

TASK:

Using the documents in your packet, your answers to the questions in Part A, and your knowledge of social studies, write a well-developed essay that includes an introduction, supporting paragraphs, and a conclusion in which you thoroughly address the following:

- Discuss at least two reasons why Americans would choose to be Loyalists and support Britain during the Revolutionary War.
- Discuss at least two reasons why Americans would choose to be Patriots and support American independence during the Revolutionary War.

NOTE: *your essay will be evaluated using the form below.*

	Point Value	Points Earned
Effective use of documents— *uses at least 5 documents*	15	_____
Accuracy— *includes correct information*	15	_____
Depth and detail— *supports main ideas with facts*	10	_____
Knowledge of social studies— *uses information beyond supplied documents*	10	_____
Clarity/Organization— *clearly expresses and logically develops ideas*	10	_____
Language mechanics— *uses proper spelling, grammar, and style*	10	_____
Correct format— *includes introduction, supporting paragraphs, and conclusion*	10	_____
TOTAL	**80**	_____

Comments: _____

_____

Part A Score _____   Part B Score _____   **TOTAL SCORE** _____

5

DBQ THEME: POLITICAL PARTIES AND THE NEW NATION

DIRECTIONS:

This task is based on the accompanying documents (1–8). Some of these documents have been edited to help you with the task. The essay is designed to test your ability to work with historical documents and your knowledge of early political parties. Carefully analyze the documents as you complete **Part A.** Your responses should help you to write the essay in **Part B.**

HISTORICAL CONTEXT:

The framers of the Constitution hoped that their new government would be free of the harmful effects of "factions," or political parties. They knew it would be hard enough to unite the country without the divisions that come with political parties. Despite this wish, parties developed anyway during the presidency of George Washington. Even though all Americans wanted the United States to succeed and grow to be a strong, prosperous nation, there were significant disagreements about the best way to make that happen.

TASK:

- Explain why political parties developed in the United States.
- Describe at least two problems caused by political parties in the early days of the United States.

PART A—SHORT-ANSWER SECTION

The following documents relate to early political parties. Examine each document carefully and answer the questions that follow.

Document 1: Differences Between Hamilton and Jefferson

ISSUES	ALEXANDER HAMILTON	THOMAS JEFFERSON
FEDERAL POWER	Hamilton wanted a strong federal government	Believed in small government - worried that a strong federal government would take power from the state governments
CONSTITUTION	He interpreted the Constitution broadly or loosely.	He believed in a strict interpretation of the Constitution.
ECONOMY	Wanted America to develop into an industrial nation.	Thought that agriculture should form the basis of the economy. He believed that industry corrupted nations.
THE NATIONAL BANK	The Bank of the United States was his idea	He believed that the National Bank was unconstitutional
FOREIGN POLICY	He wanted to develop good relations with Britain	Since they were our first ally, he supported strong ties with France
POLITICAL PARTY	Hamilton's supporter's formed the Federalist Party	Jefferson's supporters formed the Democratic-Republican Party.

Alexander Hamilton and Thomas Jefferson were two of President Washington's most talented and trusted advisors. Despite this, they agreed on very little, as the table above suggests. No two men were more responsible for America's first political parties.

1. Describe two political differences between Hamilton and Jefferson.

_____

_____

_____(2)

2. Why did Hamilton's party become known as the Federalists?

_____

_____(1)

May be copied for classroom use. *Teaching and Using Document-Based Questions for Middle School* by Edward O'Connor (Portsmouth, NH: Teacher Ideas Press); ©2004.

Document 2: Hamilton Criticizes His Opponents (1792)

It was not until the last session of Congress that I became totally convinced of the following truth: that Mr. Madison and Mr. Jefferson are at the head of a party that is hostile to me, and are acting on views that are, in my opinion, harmful to the principles of good government and dangerous to the union, peace and happiness of the country . . .

In the question concerning the Bank of the United States, Mr. Jefferson not only gave his opinion in writing that it was unconstitutional, but he did it in a style and manner which was very insulting to me . . .

In respect to foreign politics, the views of these men are in my judgment equally dangerous. They have a womanish attachment to France, and a womanish resentment towards Great Britain.

On the whole, the only enemy which the Republic has to fear is the effects of political parties. It will prevent the government from achieving its goals and create disorder so that all regular and orderly people will wish for a change, and the ones that have created the disorder will take advantage of this and seize power for themselves.

1. What are two reasons why Hamilton believes that Madison and Jefferson are dangerous?

_____

_____

_____

_____

_____(2)

2. What are two things Hamilton says in this letter that could be insulting to Jefferson?

_____

_____

_____

_____

_____(2)

Document 3: Jefferson on Parties (1797)

You may have found on your return to America a higher style of political difference than when you left here. I fear this is inseparable from the individual differences of the human mind and that degree of freedom which allows for unlimited expression. Political arguments are surely a lesser evil than the lack of thought found under tyranny, but it is still a great evil. It would be as worthy the effort of the patriot as the philosopher to avoid its influence, if possible.

1. According to Jefferson, what are two reasons for the development of political parties?

_____

_____

_____

_____

_____(2)

Document 4: Election Advertisement

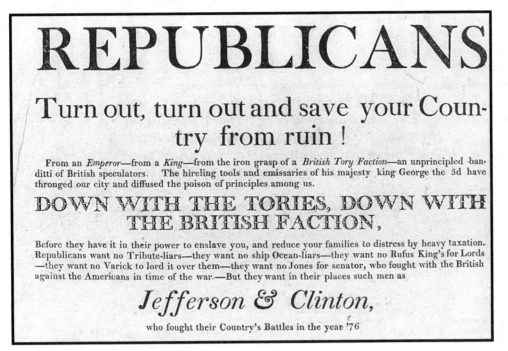

REPUBLICANS

Turn out, turn out and save your Country from ruin !

From an *Emperor*—from a *King*—from the iron grasp of a *British Tory Faction*—an unprincipled banditti of British speculators.   The hireling tools and emissaries of his majesty king George the 3d have thronged our city and diffused the poison of principles among us.

DOWN WITH THE TORIES, DOWN WITH THE BRITISH FACTION,

Before they have it in their power to enslave you, and reduce your families to distress by heavy taxation. Republicans want no Tribute-liars—they want no ship Ocean-liars—they want no Rufus King's for Lords —they want no Varick to lord it over them—they want no Jones for senator, who fought with the British against the Americans in time of the war.—But they want in their places such men as

Jefferson & Clinton,

who fought their Country's Battles in the year '76

Courtesy New-York Historical Society

One tactic that the Democratic-Republicans used to get votes was to criticize the Federalists' pro-British attitude. Republicans played upon feelings from the Revolutionary War to make people believe that Federalists were still loyal to Britain.

1. According to this advertisement, what are two things the Republicans claim about the Federalists?

_____

_____

_____

_____

_____(2)

Document 5: The Sedition Act (1798)

Be it enacted by the Senate and House of Representatives of the United States of America, in Congress assembled . . . that if any person shall write, print, speak, or publish any false, injurious or harmful writings against the government of the United States, or either House of Congress, or the President of the United States, with intent to attack the good name of the government, Congress, the President, or to bring them into disfavor or to bring about the hatred of the good people of the United States or to stir up public disorder or rebellion within the United States . . . then such a person when convicted before any court of the United States shall be punished by a fine not more than two thousand dollars, and imprisonment not more than two years.

1. Name two things a person could be punished for according to this law.

_____

_____(2)

2. How could this law make it difficult for a person to challenge a member of Congress or the

president in an election? _____

_____

_____(1)

Document 6: The Death of Alexander Hamilton (1804)

DEATH OF ALEX. HAMILTON.

Courtesy Print Collection, New York Public Library

Political parties led to more than just debate and competition. At times people grew to mistrust and even hate each other due to political differences. Aaron Burr and Alexander Hamilton grew to be bitter political rivals, eventually fighting a duel on July 11, 1804. Hamilton received a mortal wound and died early the next day.

1. How did political parties contribute to the death of Alexander Hamilton?

_____

_____

_____

_____

_____(1)

Document 7: A Letter to Massachusetts Voters (1808)

To all the voters of Massachusetts no matter of what political party they may be:

Here are short and plain reasons which all people are requested to weigh before they give their votes next Monday for Governor and Senators:
We have two parties in the state. All free governments have had and will continue to have them. Perhaps neither of them is perfectly right always, and yet, it is likely that one is more right than the other.
We shall not tell you which you are to favor, but we shall honestly state the difference in the opinions of these parties, and you must decide for yourselves. Remember, however, that your decision in this election decides your future fate.
First, there is a party to which Mr. Jefferson belongs, whose policies have had and appear still to have a tendency to drive you into an unnecessary war with Britain and bring you under the control of France.
Second, there is a peace party among whom are found Colonel Pickering, Mr. Josiah Quincy, son of the old Patriot of 1775 . . . as well as many other members of Congress and thousands of the most wise and Patriotic citizens— Mr. Gore, the candidate for governor is of this party. These men fear a war with Great Britain, because it would be a disaster, and they oppose it, because it is unnecessary . . .

1. According to this letter, what two offices will people be able to vote for in the upcoming election?

_____

_____

_____(2)

2. According to this letter, why should people vote for Mr. Gore?

_____

_____

_____(1)

Document 8: Political Cartoon—The Gerrymander (1812)

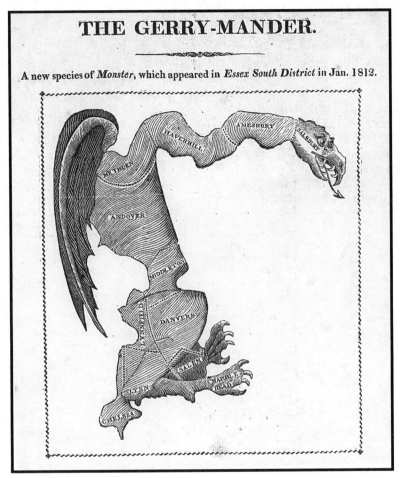

Courtesy Library of Congress

Political parties use many different methods to increase their chances of winning elections. Since election districts are created by the state governments, the party with the most power can draw them to include as many of its members as possible. This means that sometimes the boundaries can take on an unusual, even unnatural shape. The cartoon above was made to criticize Massachusetts Governor Elbridge Gerry, who used this practice to benefit his party, the Democratic-Republicans. This practice, widely regarded as undemocratic and unconstitutional, is known to this day as "gerrymandering."

1. What does the "gerrymander" represent?

_____

_____(1)

2. Why do people consider the practice of "gerrymandering" unfair?

_____

_____(1)

NAME _____ DATE _____

PART B—ESSAY: POLITICAL PARTIES AND THE NEW NATION

TASK:

Using the documents in your packet, your answers to the questions in Part A, and your knowledge of social studies, write a well-developed essay that includes an introduction, supporting paragraphs, and a conclusion in which you thoroughly address the following:

- Explain why political parties developed in the United States.
- Describe at least two problems caused by political parties in the early days of the United States.

NOTE: *your essay will be evaluated using the form below.*

	Point Value	Points Earned
Effective use of documents— *uses at least 5 documents*	15	_____
Accuracy— *includes correct information*	15	_____
Depth and detail— *supports main ideas with facts*	10	_____
Knowledge of social studies— *uses information beyond supplied documents*	10	_____
Clarity/Organization— *clearly expresses and logically develops ideas*	10	_____
Language mechanics— *uses proper spelling, grammar, and style*	10	_____
Correct format— *includes introduction, supporting paragraphs, and conclusion*	10	_____
TOTAL	**80**	_____

Comments: _____

_____

_____

Part A Score _____   Part B Score _____   **TOTAL SCORE** _____

6

DBQ THEME: DIFFERENCES BETWEEN THE NORTH AND THE SOUTH

DIRECTIONS:

This task is based on the accompanying documents (1–9). Some of these documents have been edited to help you with the task. The essay is designed to test your ability to work with historical documents and your knowledge of the developing differences between the North and the South. Carefully analyze the documents as you complete **Part A**. Your responses should help you to write the essay in **Part B**.

HISTORICAL CONTEXT:

Conflict between the northern and southern states began long before the Civil War; in fact, the roots of the problem go back as far as colonial times. The North and the South developed differently in many ways: socially, economically, and even politically in some respects. The differences between them grew greater during the early years of the republic, as their distrust of each other became increasingly intense.

TASK:

- Discuss at least two economic differences between the North and the South before the Civil War.

- Discuss at least two political arguments that occurred between the North and the South before the Civil War.

PART A—SHORT-ANSWER SECTION

The following documents relate to differences between the North and the South. Examine each document carefully and answer the questions that follow.

Document 1: Colonial Slave Imports

SLAVES IMPORTED TO SELECTED COLONIES 1768-1772											
Year	NH	MA	RI	CT	NY	PA	MD	VA	NC	SC	GA
1772	4	4	2	0	23	0	175	2,104	155	7,201	328
1771	0	0	12	0	9	0	227	762	82	3,100	758
1770	0	0	0	0	69	0	532	905	115	123	1,144
1769	4	0	6	0	0	10	203	493	169	4,888	687
1768	12	0	70	14	19	0	301	354	198	249	1,001

Note: colony abbreviations:

NH—New Hampshire   MA—Massachusetts   RI—Rhode Island
CT—Connecticut   NY—New York   PA—Pennsylvania
MD—Maryland   VA—Virginia   NC—North Carolina
SC—South Carolina   GA—Georgia

Source: Historical Statistics of the United States

1. Which colony imported the most slaves?

_____

_____(1)

2. Which colony imported the fewest slaves?

_____

_____(1)

3. What is the difference between northern and southern imports of slaves during the years

1768–1772? _____

_____

_____(1)

May be copied for classroom use. *Teaching and Using Document-Based Questions for Middle School* by Edward O'Connor (Portsmouth, NH: Teacher Ideas Press); ©2004.

Document 2: A Letter from Thomas Jefferson to John Adams (1812)

Here we do little in the fine way, but a great deal of coarse and decent goods. Every family in the country is a manufactory within itself, and is very able to make for itself all the decent things for its own clothing and household use. We consider a sheep for every person in the family as sufficient to clothe it, and in addition to the cotton, hemp and flax which we raise ourselves. For finer things we shall depend on your northern manufacturers. Of these companies we have none. We use little machinery. The Spinning Jenny and loom can be managed in a family; but nothing more complicated.

1. Name two materials that people in Jefferson's state (Virginia) use to make clothing.

_____

_____

_____

_____(2)

2. What is the difference between how goods are made in Virginia and Massachusetts, Adams's home

state? _____

_____

_____

_____(1)

Document 3: Observations of a French Visitor to America (1831)

The stream that the Indians named the Ohio, or Beautiful River, waters one of the most magnificent valleys in which man has ever lived. On both banks of the Ohio stretched rolling ground which offers the farmer unending treasures; on both banks the air is equally healthy and the climate temperate. The land on the left bank is called Kentucky, the other takes its name from the river itself. There is but one difference between the two states: Kentucky allows slaves, but Ohio refuses to have them.

On the left bank of the Ohio work is connected with the idea of slavery, but on the right with well-being and progress. On the one side it is humiliating, but on the other honorable. On the left bank no white laborers are to be found, for they would be afraid of being like slaves. For work, people must rely on the Negroes. One will never see a man of leisure on the right bank: the white man's intelligent activity is used for work of every sort.

Slavery, which is abolished in the North, still exists in the South. Trade and industry are bound to flourish more in the North than in the South. It is natural that both population and wealth should pile up there more quickly.

Source: Alexis de Tocqueville,
Democracy in America

1. According to the author, what is a harmful effect of slavery?

_____

_____

_____

_____(1)

2. According to the author, how does the North benefit from refusing slavery?

_____

_____

_____

_____(1)

Document 4: A Cotton Plantation on the Mississippi

Courtesy Library of Congress

1. What kind of work are the people in this picture doing?

_____

_____

_____

_____(1)

2. Describe the people who are doing the work in this picture.

_____

_____

_____

_____(1)

Document 5: A Description of Lowell, Massachusetts (1845)

The Lowell bank—the first in town—was established March 11, 1828. That same year two new manufacturing companies were started—the Appleton and Lowell—both of which immediately started to build mills. A vast increase of the business of Lowell was planned in 1830, by the construction of the Western Suffolk Canal. This was dug in 1831 and 1832. Instead of using the whole waterfall of thirty-two feet at once, it was proposed to divide it into two falls of sixteen feet each; and thus power was obtained for three new companies. The Suffolk, Tremont, and Lawrence companies were established in spring of 1831, and right away began building mills and boarding houses for their workers. A bleaching company was established in 1832. Still another canal was dug in 1835, to carry water to the mills of the Boott Company, which put up five large factories and eight blocks of boarding houses.

The money here invested in manufacturing is twelve million dollars. There are made in Lowell, every week, 1,459,001 yards of cloth amounting to 75,868,000 yards per year. This is nearly enough to belt the globe two times around. 61,100 bales of cotton are worked up every year.

1. What was used to power the mills at Lowell?

_____

_____

_____

_____

_____(1)

2. What are two things in this passage that suggest that businesses were successful in Lowell?

_____

_____

_____

_____

_____(2)

Document 6: A View of Pittsburgh, Pennsylvania

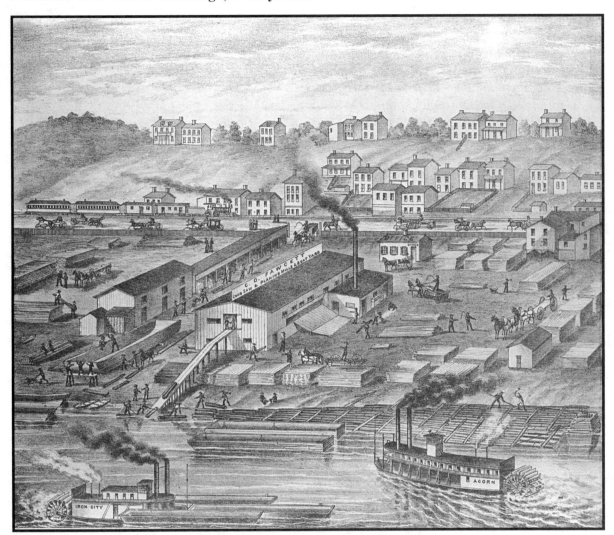

Courtesy Library of Congress

1. What are two methods of transportation shown in this picture?

_____

_____

_____(2)

2. Describe two types of work being done in this picture.

_____

_____(2)

Document 7: A Speech by Senator Robert Young Hayne of South Carolina (1830)

The purpose of the authors of the Constitution was not to strengthen the government, but to strengthen the Union. It was not to draw power from the States in order to transfer it to a national government, but in the language of the Constitution itself, "to form a more perfect Union".

Who, then, are the true friends of the Union? Those who would limit the federal government strictly within the limits outlined in the Constitution; who would preserve for the States the powers not specifically given to the federal government. And who are its enemies? Those who are in favor of strengthening the federal government; who are constantly stealing power from the States, and adding to the strength of the federal government.

The idea that the federal government is able to judge the extent and limits of its own power seems to go completely against the independence of the States. If the federal government alone can determine the limits of its own authority, and the States are forced to go along with these decisions, without being allowed to decide for themselves when the Constitution has been overstepped, then this is practically a government with unlimited powers.

1. According to Senator Hayne, what was the purpose of the Constitution?

_____

_____

_____

_____(1)

2. What is Senator Hayne's main concern in this passage?

_____

_____

_____

_____(1)

Document 8: Massachusetts Senator Daniel Webster's Response to Hayne (1830)

Sir, what is this danger, and what are the grounds for it? Let it be remembered that the Constitution of the United States is changeable. It is to continue in its present form no longer than the people shall choose to have it. If they shall decide that they have unfairly divided power between the States and the federal government, they can change that division at will. But while the people choose to keep the Constitution as it is, while they are satisfied with it and refuse to change it, why should the State legislatures have the right to change it?

But sir, although there are fears, there are hopes also. The people have preserved this, their chosen Constitution, for forty years, and have seen their happiness and prosperity grow. They are now strongly attached to it. It cannot be overthrown by attack; it will not be undermined or nullified.

I admit that in my career up to now I have kept steadily in view the prosperity and honor of the whole country, and the preservation of our Federal Union. It is to that Union that we owe our safety at home and our dignity among other nations. It is to that Union that we are chiefly indebted for whatever makes us most proud of our country.

1. According to Webster, why shouldn't Senator Hayne worry about the power of the federal government?

_____

_____

_____

_____(1)

2. According to Webster, what are two ways that Americans benefit from the structure of the federal

government? _____

_____

_____

_____(2)

Document 9: South Carolina's Ordinance of Nullification (1832)

The Congress of the United States by various acts, supposedly to put taxes and duties on imports of foreign goods, but in reality intended for the protection of Northern manufactures, has exceeded its just powers under the Constitution. That document allows Congress no powers to give such protection. Congress has also violated the true meaning of the Constitution, which calls for equality in imposing taxes upon the States.

We, therefore, the people of the State of South Carolina in convention assembled, declare that the acts of Congress which impose taxes on imports of foreign goods, and more specifically the Tariffs of 1828 and 1832, are unauthorized by the Constitution of the United States and therefore are null, void and are not law, nor binding upon this State or its citizens.

1. What are two reasons why South Carolina claimed the Tariffs of 1828 and 1832 were

unconstitutional? _____

_____

_____

_____

_____(2)

2. How would this ordinance affect the people of South Carolina?

_____

_____

_____

_____

_____(1)

NAME _____ DATE _____

PART B—ESSAY: DIFFERENCES BETWEEN THE NORTH AND THE SOUTH

TASK:

Using the documents in your packet, your answers to the questions in Part A, and your knowledge of social studies, write a well-developed essay that includes an introduction, supporting paragraphs, and a conclusion in which you thoroughly address the following:

- Discuss at least two economic differences between the North and the South before the Civil War.
- Discuss at least two political arguments that occurred between the North and the South before the Civil War.

NOTE: *your essay will be evaluated using the form below.*

	Point Value	Points Earned
Effective use of documents— *uses at least 5 documents*	15	_____
Accuracy— *includes correct information*	10	_____
Depth and detail— *supports main ideas with facts*	10	_____
Knowledge of social studies— *uses information beyond supplied documents*	10	_____
Clarity/Organization— *clearly expresses and logically develops ideas*	10	_____
Language mechanics— *uses proper spelling, grammar, and style*	10	_____
Correct format— *includes introduction, supporting paragraphs, and conclusion*	10	_____
TOTAL	75	_____

Comments: _____

_____

_____

Part A Score _____   Part B Score _____   **TOTAL SCORE** _____

7

DBQ THEME:
SLAVERY IN THE UNITED STATES

DIRECTIONS:

This task is based on the accompanying documents (1–9). Some of these documents have been edited to help you with the task. The essay is designed to test your ability to work with historical documents and your knowledge of slavery. Carefully analyze the documents as you complete **Part A**. Your responses should help you to write the essay in **Part B**.

HISTORICAL CONTEXT:

From the earliest colonial times to 1865, slavery existed in the United States. During that time, millions of men, women, and children were denied almost all basic human rights. Slaves had no freedom, no power to control their own lives, no ability to protect family members from harsh treatment, no means to keep their families together. Many of the human rights that slaves were made to live without are so basic that free people often take them for granted. It is important for Americans in the twenty-first century to study this period of our history and understand how people could inflict such hardship and injustice on others.

TASK:

- Describe the ways in which slaves were denied their basic human rights.

- Explain at least two reasons why slaveholders denied slaves their basic human rights.

PART A—SHORT-ANSWER SECTION

The following documents relate to slavery in America. Examine each document carefully and answer the questions that follow.

Document 1: A Speech by Frederick Douglass (1850)

> *A master is a person who claims and exercises a right of property in the person of his fellow man. He does this with the force of law and the blessing of Southern religion. The law gives the master absolute power over the slave. He may work him, hire him out, sell him, and in certain circumstances, kill him . . . The slave is a person without any rights . . . his name is disrespectfully inserted in the master's account book, with horses, sheep and pigs. In law, the slave has no wife, no children, and no home. He can own nothing, possess nothing, acquire nothing, but what must belong to another. To eat the fruit of his own labor is considered stealing . . .*
>
> *To ensure good behavior, the slaveholder relies on the whip; to make the slave humble, he relies on the whip; to take the place of wages as motivation to work, he relies on the whip; to destroy his manhood he relies on the whip, the chain, the gag, the thumb-screw, the pillory, the knife, the pistol and the bloodhound. These are the necessary parts of the system . . .*

1. Name at least two human rights that are denied to slaves, according to Frederick Douglass.

_____

_____

_____

_____(2)

2. Give two reasons why slaveholders would beat their slaves.

_____

_____

_____

_____(2)

May be copied for classroom use. *Teaching and Using Document-Based Questions for Middle School* by Edward O'Connor (Portsmouth, NH: Teacher Ideas Press); ©2004.

Document 2: Auction Advertisement (1860)

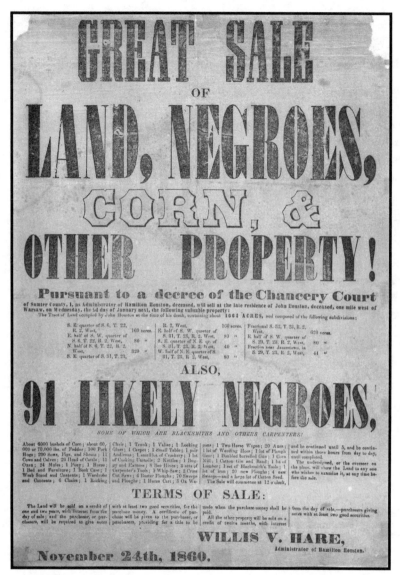

Courtesy Gilder Lehrman Institute of American History, New York, NY

1. Besides slaves, what are two other items being sold at this auction?

_____

_____(2)

2. What does this advertisement suggest about slaveholders' opinion of African Americans?

_____

_____(1)

Document 3: Georgia Asks for Slavery (1738)

The colony of Georgia was founded in 1732, and the leaders of the colony decided in 1735 that slavery should be illegal there. Many colonists were unhappy about this decision and requested a change in this policy several times. Georgia eventually accepted slavery in 1749.

> *At this time, timber is the only thing we have here which we can export and only because we have to cut it down for planting our land, yet we cannot manufacture it for a foreign market, but at double the expense of the other colonies; for instance, in South Carolina, which is only twenty miles from us, because they are allowed to use Negroes, can load vessels with that product at one half of the price that we can do; and what would convince persons to bring ships here, when they can be loaded with one half the expense so near us? Therefore, the timber on the land is only a problem to those that have it, though of very great value in all the other colonies where Negroes are allowed, and therefore labor is cheap.*
>
> *It is very well known that the Carolinas can raise everything that this colony can, and because their labor is so much cheaper, they will always ruin our business . . .*

1. According to this document, why do the citizens of Georgia want slavery?

_____

_____(1)

2. Name at least one job that slaves would be doing in Georgia, according to this document.

_____(1)

Document 4: Voyage to America on a Slave Ship

I was soon put down under the decks, where I was met with the most terrible odor. With the stench and crying together, I became so sick and low that I was not able to eat, nor had I the least desire to taste anything. But soon, to my grief, two of the white men offered me food, and upon my refusing to eat, one of them held me fast by the hands and tied my feet, while the other whipped me severely. I had never experienced anything like this before, and although I feared the water, if I were able to get over the nettings, I would have jumped over the side, but I could not . . .

One day, when we had a smooth sea and moderate wind, two of my wearied countrymen, who were chained together, preferring death to a life of misery, somehow made it through the nettings and jumped into the sea. Immediately another quite dejected fellow, who on account of his illness was allowed to be out of irons, also followed their example. There was such a noise and confusion among the people of the ship to stop and get the boat to go after the slaves. Two of the wretches were drowned, but they got the other, and afterwards whipped him unmercifully for preferring death to slavery.

1. Why did some of the people jump overboard?

_____

_____(1)

Document 5: Devices of Slavery

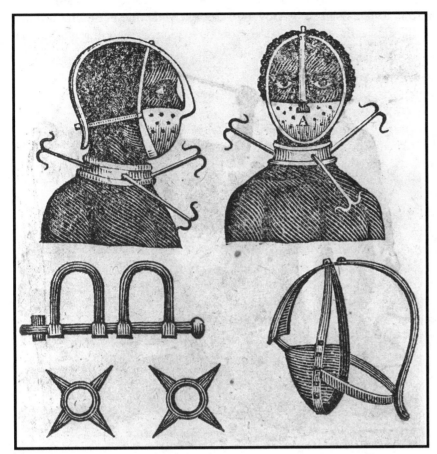

Courtesy Library of Congress

The illustration above includes an iron mask and collar, which were sometimes used by slaveholders. The collar was designed to prevent field workers from running away and the mask made it impossible for them to eat the crops they were raising. All of these devices caused pain to those who were forced to wear them.

1. Name two reasons why slaves were forced to use the iron mask and collar?

_____

_____

_____(2)

2. Why were these devices unpleasant for slaves to wear?

_____

_____

_____(1)

Document 6: A Speech Defending Slavery (1835)

The following passage is taken from a speech given by Governor George McDuffie of South Carolina. The speech was given to the state legislature in response to the growing evidence of abolitionists in that state.

> *No human institution, in my opinion, is more clearly consistent with the will of God than slavery. That the African Negro is destined to occupy this condition of servitude is not less clear. It is marked on the face, stamped on the skin, and shown by the inferiority of this race. They have all the qualities that fit them to be slaves, and not one of those that would fit them to be free men. Until the "African can change his skin," it will be useless to try by any human power, to make free men of those whom God has doomed to be slaves . . .*
>
> *Other consequences of freeing slaves may be shown to every abolitionist in Europe or America. It is clearly shown that the production of cotton depends, not so much on soil and climate as on the existence of slavery. In the places where it grows, not one half the quantity would be produced but for the existence of slavery; and every realistic planter will agree in the opinion that if all the slaves in these states were now freed, the American crop would be reduced the very next year from 1,200,000 to 600,000 bales.*

1. What was McDuffie's economic argument for slavery?

_____

_____

_____

_____

_____(1)

2. What was McDuffie's racial argument for slavery?

_____

_____

_____

_____

_____(1)

SLAVERY IN THE UNITED STATES

Document 7: Keeping Slave Families Together

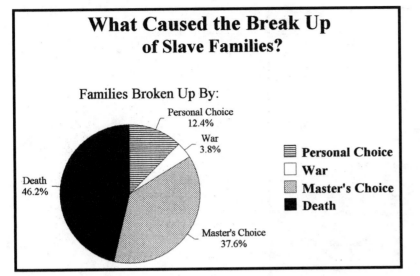

Source: Blasingame, John W., The Slave Community

The data above are based on a sample from Mississippi, Tennessee, and Louisiana. Of the 2,888 families included in the survey, 2,494 (86%) were broken up by one of the four factors listed above.

1. What are the two main reasons for the break-up of slave families?

_____

_____

_____

_____(2)

2. What can be said about the part the master played in the break-up of slave families?

_____

_____

_____

_____(1)

Document 8: Photograph of a Slave Who Was Whipped (1863)

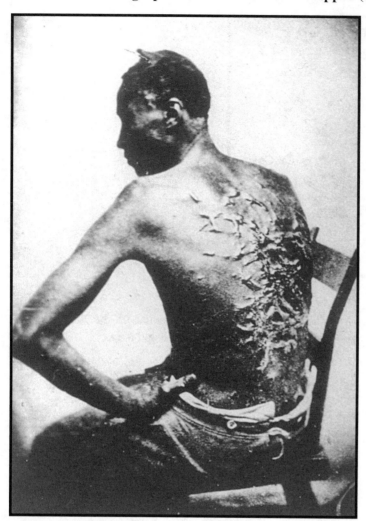

Courtesy National Archives

Beatings with a whip were a common form of punishment used on slaves. The slave shown above was unable to work for two months after receiving the beating that left these scars on his back.

1. What does this photograph suggest about how slaves were treated?

_____

_____

_____

_____(1)

Document 9: Description of a Slave Auction

Little Randall was made to jump and run across the floor, demonstrating his activity and condition. All the time the trade was going on Eliza was crying aloud, and wringing her hands. She begged the man not to buy him, unless he also bought herself and her daughter Emily. She promised, in that case, to be the most faithful slave that ever lived. The man answered that he could not afford it, and Eliza burst into grief . . . She wanted to be with her children, she said. . . . Over and over again she told them how she loved her boy. But it was of no avail; the man could not afford it. The bargain was agreed upon, and Randall must go alone. Then Eliza ran to him, embraced him passionately, kissed him again and again and told him to remember her—all the while her tears falling in the boy's face like rain. "Don't cry mama. I will be a good boy. Don't cry," said Randall, looking back as they passed out of the door. What became of the lad, God knows.

1. Explain why Eliza couldn't keep her family together.

_____

_____

_____

_____(1)

NAME _____ DATE _____

PART B—ESSAY: SLAVERY IN THE UNITED STATES

TASK:

Using the documents in your packet, your answers to the questions in Part A, and your knowledge of social studies, write a well-developed essay that includes an introduction, supporting paragraphs, and a conclusion in which you thoroughly address the following:

- Describe the ways in which slaves were denied their basic human rights.
- Explain at least two reasons why slaveholders denied slaves their basic human rights.

NOTE: *your essay will be evaluated using the form below.*

	Point Value	Points Earned
Effective use of documents— *uses at least 5 documents*	15	_____
Accuracy— *includes correct information*	15	_____
Depth and detail— *supports main ideas with facts*	10	_____
Knowledge of social studies— *uses information beyond supplied documents*	10	_____
Clarity/Organization— *clearly expresses and logically develops ideas*	10	_____
Language mechanics— *uses proper spelling, grammar, and style*	10	_____
Correct format— *includes introduction, supporting paragraphs, and conclusion*	10	_____
TOTAL	**80**	_____

Comments:_____

_____

_____

Part A Score _____   Part B Score _____   **TOTAL SCORE** _____

8

DBQ THEME: RECONSTRUCTION

DIRECTIONS:

This task is based on the accompanying documents (1–8). Some of these documents have been edited to help you with the task. The essay is designed to test your ability to work with historical documents and your knowledge of Reconstruction. Carefully analyze the documents as you complete **Part A**. Your responses should help you to write the essay in **Part B**.

HISTORICAL CONTEXT:

The period of time from the end of the Civil War (1865) until 1877 is known as Reconstruction. This was a period of tremendous change, during which the nation faced many difficult problems. Besides rebuilding cities and towns that were destroyed during the long and costly war, people who were rebels had to be brought back into the Union, over 4 million former slaves and their former masters needed to adjust to emancipation, and the South faced serious economic problems. The United States met with many successes during Reconstruction, but it also committed many failures in trying to reunite the divided nation.

TASK:

- Describe at least three major changes that took place in the United States during Reconstruction.
- Describe at least two successes of Reconstruction.
- Describe at least two failures of Reconstruction.

PART A—SHORT-ANSWER SECTION

The following documents relate to Reconstruction. Examine each document carefully and answer the questions that follow.

Document 1: A Southerner Describes Politics During Reconstruction

Congress passed an act by which registration was required of all male citizens in South Carolina, and an election of delegates by them to a State Constitutional convention. The election was held under the protection of the military commander of the district, General Dan Sickles.

When the registration was completed, it showed a Negro majority. Then it looked like every sharp cunning rascal who could get a carpetbag and transportation from above the Mason Dixon line put out to the State in quest of political adventure.

These carpetbaggers and a few South Carolina white scalawags organized the Federal Union Republican Party and laid plans to control the Constitutional Convention of 1868. They accomplished their purpose.

The Convention met in Charleston in 1868, composed of twenty-three scalawags, twenty-five carpetbaggers and seventy-six Negroes. As they know nothing about society and constitutional law, it is a wonder they gave us a constitution as good as they did. It was modeled after the State Constitution of Ohio. We lived under its provisions until 1895. Overall, it was an improvement from the constitutions of 1795 and 1865, in that it prohibited imprisonment for debt; divided up representation in the House of Representatives according to the numbers of people living in a county; provided for the public free school system; and required attendance of all children ages six to sixteen . . .

1. Name at least two groups of people that were involved in creating the Constitution of South Carolina.

_____

_____

_____(2)

2. What were two positive features of the Constitution of 1868, according to the author?

_____

_____

_____(2)

May be copied for classroom use. *Teaching and Using Document-Based Questions for Middle School* by Edward O'Connor (Portsmouth, NH: Teacher Ideas Press); ©2004.

Document 2: Illustration: "Everything Points to a Democratic Victory this Fall" (1874)

Courtesy Library of Congress

Even though Freedmen were granted the right to vote with the Fifteenth Amendment, southern whites found ways to prevent African Americans from voting, as suggested by the illustration above. Without Freedmen's votes, the traditional party of the South, the Democratic party, was able to regain control of southern politics.

1. What are two ways shown in this illustration that Freedmen were prevented from voting?

_____

_____

_____

_____(2)

Document 3: A Freedman Describes His Experience

Continuing to enjoy good health and obtaining steady work, we had saved enough money within two years to buy the house and lot, having nearly two-thirds cash therefor. I felt proud, being then for the first time in my life a land owner, but it was of short duration. I had relied upon the word of a white man, and had paid him the amount agreed upon, and had received what I had supposed to be a clear title to the land, but it turned out soon afterwards, that the man owned only the house, and the land upon which it stood was the property of another, who notified me to pay rent for the land or move my house away.

In thus describing my own experience upon being freed from slavery, I only show that of over four million others. History does not show where four millions of people had been held in slavery so long, that they had lost all knowledge of the way to provide for their own support, to spend their earnings to advantage, to use economy in buying necessities of life and to save up for another day.

This was the condition of the Colored people at the end of the war. They were set free without a dollar, without a foot of land, and without the ability to get the next meal, and this too, by a great nation.

It does seem to me, that a great nation, which had received such wealth from the labor of an enslaved people, upon setting them free, would at least, have given them a square meal. Justice seems to demand one year's support, forty acres and a mule each.

Did they get any portion of it? Not a cent. Four million people turned loose without a dollar and told to "Root hog or die!" Now whose duty was it to feed them? My opinion is that the government should have done it.

1. What are two problems the author faced after being freed?

_____

_____

_____(2)

2. List at least one criticism of the government expressed by the author.

_____

_____

_____

_____(1)

Document 4: Sharecropping

Courtesy Library of Congress

After the Civil War, freed men and women had no money, no land, and very few skills. Many former slaves became sharecroppers, sometimes even on the plantations owned by their former masters. Share-croppers farmed on land they rented from a landlord, in exchange for a share of the crop they produced. Because sharecroppers needed to borrow money for necessities like tools and food, they seldom were able to make or save any money. Pictured above is a sharecropper working in a cotton field.

1. Name two ways that sharecropping was similar to slavery.

_____

_____

_____(2)

Document 5: "Worse Than Slavery" (1874)

Courtesy Library of Congress

This illustration appeared in *Harper's Weekly* in October, 1874, and depicted conditions faced by African Americans in the South at the time.

1. According to this illustration, who is responsible for making freedom "Worse Than Slavery" for

African Americans? _____

_____

_____(2)

2. Name at least two things that African Americans experienced according to this illustration.

_____

_____(2)

Document 6: A Tennessee Family Moves West

My folks were natives of Tennessee, and lived in Lawrence County, at which place I was born. My father's name was James D. Riley. He owned and operated a plantation, also, was engaged in diverse other kinds of business. At the beginning of the Civil War, he was considered a wealthy man, but at the conclusion of the war, he was a financial wreck, as many others in the Southern states were.

He decided to improve his financial position in Texas and migrated to that state in 1877. We traveled to Dallas by train, which was the end of the railroad for a passenger at that date.

From Dallas we traveled overland in a covered wagon pulled by a team of horses, to Mill County, where my father bought a tract of land. On this land we established a home and engaged in farming, also ranged a few cattle on the open range.

The main factor which caused father to settle in Mill County was that a colony of Tennessee folks was located there.

1. Why did the Riley family move from Tennessee to Texas?

_____

_____

_____(1)

Document 7: Schools for Freedmen

Courtesy Library of Congress

Before the Civil War, it was considered a crime for a slave to learn how to read and write, so it is not surprising that schools were considered to be a priority by many people after Emancipation. The illustration above shows a school for Freedmen in Mississippi.

1. Name at least one thing that the students in this illustration are doing that they could not do as

slaves. _____

_____

_____

_____ (1)

Document 8: "A Yankee Visits the New South" (1887)

When we come to the New Industrial South, the change is marvelous. . . . Instead of a South devoted to agriculture and politics, we find a South wide awake to business, excited and astonished at the development of its own immense resources . . .

The South is manufacturing a great variety of things needed in the house, on the farm and in the shops, and already sends to the North and West several manufactured products. The most striking industrial development today is in iron, coal, lumber, and marble. More encouraging for the Southern people is the multiplication of small industries in nearly every city I visited.

It cannot be too strongly impressed upon the public mind that the South, to use an understandable phrase, "has joined the procession." Its mind is turned to the development of its resources, to business, to enterprise, to education, to economic problems; it is marching with the North in the same purpose of wealth by industry. It is true that the railways, mines, and furnaces could not have been without huge investments of Northern money, but I was continually surprised to find so many and important local industries the result of Southern funds, made and saved since the war.

1. According to this article, what is the great change that has occurred in the new South?

_____

_____

_____

_____

_____(1)

2. Name at least two products or resources of the new South.

_____

_____

_____(2)

PART B—ESSAY: RECONSTRUCTION

TASK:

Using the documents in your packet, your answers to the questions in Part A, and your knowledge of social studies, write a well-developed essay that includes an introduction, supporting paragraphs, and a conclusion in which you thoroughly address the following:

- Describe at least three major changes that took place in the United States during Reconstruction.
- Describe at least two successes of Reconstruction.
- Describe at least two failures of Reconstruction.

NOTE: *your essay will be evaluated using the form below.*

	Point Value	Points Earned
Effective use of documents— *uses at least 5 documents*	15	_____
Accuracy— *includes correct information*	15	_____
Depth and detail— *supports main ideas with facts*	10	_____
Knowledge of social studies— *uses information beyond supplied documents*	10	_____
Clarity/Organization— *clearly expresses and logically develops ideas*	10	_____
Language mechanics— *uses proper spelling, grammar, and style*	10	_____
Correct format— *includes introduction, supporting paragraphs, and conclusion*	10	_____
TOTAL	**80**	_____

Comments: _____

_____

_____

Part A Score _____   Part B Score _____   **TOTAL SCORE** _____

9

DBQ Theme: Immigration

DIRECTIONS:

This task is based on the accompanying documents (1–9). Some of these documents have been edited to help you with the task. The essay is designed to test your ability to work with historical documents and your knowledge of immigration. Carefully analyze the documents as you complete **Part A**. Your responses should help you to write the essay in **Part B**.

HISTORICAL CONTEXT:

America is a land of immigrants. From colonial times to the present, people have come to America for the many freedoms and opportunities that exist here. The nineteenth and twentieth centuries saw tremendous waves of immigrants flock to the United States from many different nations. Although many people in America opposed immigration and called for its restriction, the immigrants had a major impact on America.

TASK:

- Describe at least three ways in which immigrants contributed to life in America.
- Discuss at least two reasons why many Americans were opposed to immigration.

PART A—SHORT-ANSWER SECTION

The following documents relate to immigration. Examine each document carefully and answer the questions that follow.

Document 1: An Argument for Immigration (Thomas L. Nichols 1845)

> *It is not money alone that adds to the wealth of a country, but every day's productive labor. Every house built, every canal dug, every railroad graded, has added so much to the actual wealth of society; and who have built more houses, dug more canals, or graded more railroads than the hardy Irishmen? I hardly know how our great national works could have been carried on without them; while every pair of sturdy arms has added to our national wealth, every hungry mouth has been a home market for our agriculture, and every broad shoulder has been clothed with our manufactures.*
>
> *America gets from Europe the most valuable of her people. It is the strong minded, the brave hearted, the free and self-respecting, the enterprising and intelligent, who break away from all the ties of country and of home, and brave the dangers of the ocean in search of liberty and independence for themselves and their children.*

Thomas L. Nichols was a doctor, historian and journalist in the nineteenth century.

1. According to this passage, what are two ways America benefits from immigration?

_____

_____

_____

_____(2)

2. According to Nichols, what characteristics do immigrants usually have?

_____

_____

_____

_____(1)

May be copied for classroom use. *Teaching and Using Document-Based Questions for Middle School* by Edward O'Connor (Portsmouth, NH: Teacher Ideas Press); ©2004.

Document 2: A Senator Speaks Out Against Immigration (1849)

The danger, though great, is not totally without a cure. We can do something if we do it quickly. The German and Slavic races are combining in the State of New York to elect candidates of their own blood to Congress. This is the beginning of a conflict of the races on a large scale.

Look at the great numbers who are constantly pouring into the northwestern states from Germany, making large and exclusive settlements for themselves, which in a few years will number thousands and tens of thousands, living in isolation, speaking a strange language, having foreign manners, habits, opinions, and religious faiths, knowing nothing of our political system; all handed down to their children through generations. In less than fifty years, northern Illinois, parts of Ohio, and Michigan, Wisconsin, Iowa, and Minnesota will be possessed by them; they will number millions and millions, and they will be a separate people, a nation within a nation, a new Germany.

This speech was given by Senator Garrett Davis of Kentucky.

1. According to Senator Davis, what are two problems created by immigrants?

_____

_____

_____

_____(2)

Document 3: Chinese Laborers, Humboldt Plains Nevada (1868)

Courtesy Union Pacific Railroad

1. What kind of work are these Chinese immigrants doing?

_____

_____

_____

_____(1)

Document 4: Memoir of David P. Conyngham, Civil War Soldier (1866)

The Irish people in New York and throughout the Northern States were not slow in siding with the Union and volunteering for its defense.

The Irish felt that not only was the safety of the great Republic, the home of their exiled race, at stake, but also the great principles of democracy were at issue. The Irish soldier felt that the safety and welfare of his adopted country and its glorious Constitution were in danger; he therefore willingly threw himself into the fight to support the flag that sheltered him when he was persecuted and forced to leave his own country, the laws that protected him, and the country that, like a loving mother poured forth richness to aid him.

The Irish soldier was a patriot. He had just the same right to fight for America that the native born American had. The Irish, the German, the Pole, and all other immigrants have an interest in the maintenance of the American Union.

Capt. David P. Conyngham was a staff officer of the "Irish Brigade".

1. What are two things the Irish were fighting for, according to Conyngham?

_____

_____

_____

_____

_____(2)

2. According to this passage, why did the Irish feel they owed America their support?

_____

_____

_____

_____(1)

Document 5: Comments about Immigration in *Atlantic Monthly* (October 1900)

Since it is one of the strongest instincts of human nature to dislike what is different from one's self, or what one is not familiar with, and since another instinct is to blame someone else for one's own troubles, it is not surprising that from the very day our own families arrived here as immigrants we have objected to the coming of other immigrants. It is also no surprise that we have blamed them for various problems that have arisen from time to time in industry, politics and society.

Each day's news gives us some new item to strengthen and confirm these ideas. Now a great strike, now a fight in a tenement house in which some heads are broken, now the turning of an election against our party or candidate, is one more bit of evidence to our minds that the foreigner is the root of all evil.

That we think the later comers inferior in quality to earlier immigrants may be because they are really inferior. But it may be because a slow change to a better opinion of those that came earlier has been going on.

Familiarity has certainly had much to do with our general acceptance of the Germans. This people whom we rely upon today as among our most valued citizens, our grandfathers thought of as all that was dangerous and bad.

1. According to this article, what are two reasons why some people dislike immigrants?

_____

_____

_____

_____

_____(2)

2. According to this article, why has people's opinion of Germans changed?

_____

_____

_____

_____(1)

Document 6: Political Cartoon (1893)

LOOKING BACKWARD.
They Would Close to the New-Comer the Bridge that Carried Them and their Fathers Over.

Courtesy Prints Collection, New York Public Library

"LOOKING BACKWARD. They would close to the newcomer the bridge that carried them and their fathers over."

1. What do the shadows behind the wealthy men represent?

_____

_____

_____(1)

2. Why don't the wealthy men want the immigrant to come into the United States?

_____

_____

_____(1)

Document 7: *The Immigrant Invasion* (1913)

One view of immigration is obvious to the worker who has been driven out of his position by the immigrant; to those who see the disastrous effects upon the American worker of this foreign stream of cheap labor; to those personally familiar with the poverty in many of our foreign "colonies"; to those who know of the congested slum districts in our large industrial centers and cities.

At the present time there is a surplus of cheap labor—a greater supply than our industries and manufacturing need. Employment is controlled by the more recent immigrant, because of his immediate necessity to gain employment, and his ability to sell his labor at a low price—to work for a low wage. In the face of this, the native born American and the earlier immigrant cannot defend themselves. It is causing great harm to the standard of living of hundreds of thousands of workers, who are also citizens, fathers, and husbands.

1. According to this passage, why is it easy for immigrants to find jobs?

_____

_____

_____

_____

_____(1)

2. What impact did immigrants have on the United States, according to the author?

_____

_____

_____

_____

_____(1)

Document 8: Chart—Well-Known Immigrants

A SAMPLE OF AMERICA'S WELL KNOWN IMMIGRANTS			
IMMIGRANT	**KNOWN FOR**	**NATION**	**YEAR**
Charles Atlas	Body building	Italy	1923
Irving Berlin	Song writer (example: "God Bless America")	Russia	1893
Frank Capra	Movie director (example: "It's A Wonderful Life")	Italy	1903
Frank Costello	Gangster	Italy	1893
Albert Einstein	Scientist – nuclear physics	Germany	1933
Felix Frankfurter	U. S. Supreme Court Justice	Austria	1894
Marcus Garvey	Founder-Universal Negro Improvement Association	Jamaica	1916
Charles "Lucky" Luciano	Gangster	Italy	1906
Jacob Riis	Social reformer and author	Denmark	1870
Knute Rockne	Football coach: University of Notre Dame	Norway	1893

1. Name one immigrant who served in the United States government.

_____

_____

_____

_____

_____(1)

Document 9: "A Jewish Search for Freedom"

The vast migrations from Eastern Europe created the Jewish ghettos on the Lower East Side of Manhattan. But whoever our neighbors were and no matter from where they came, they had, like my parents, come with bundles, bags, old books, downy pillows, feather comforters in red-pink coverings, copper pots, candlesticks for the Sabbath, and menorahs for lighting up a golden holiday.

All of them were seeking the "Golden Land"—within a few square miles of the Lower East Side. But what they found became New York's triumphs and tragedies of reckless architecture, sudden slums, terrible factories—and the high rises that symbolize the rush and hurry . . . They had come in a hurry in the holds of ships, to build the Medina of the New World. They had come from something much worse, but between 1900 and 1970 they and their sons contributed much of what we have today, including the garment industry, the jewelry trades, the retail shops, the current medical and dental professions, and some of New York's searing landscape.

1. What did Jewish immigrants to New York City have in common?

_____

_____

_____

_____

_____(1)

2. What are two contributions made by Jewish immigrants and their descendants?

_____

_____

_____

_____(2)

NAME _____ DATE _____

PART B—ESSAY: IMMIGRATION

TASK:

Using the documents in your packet, your answers to the questions in Part A, and your knowledge of social studies, write a well-developed essay that includes an introduction, supporting paragraphs, and a conclusion in which you thoroughly address the following:

- Describe at least three ways in which immigrants affected life in America.
- Discuss at least two reasons why many Americans were opposed to immigration.

NOTE: *your essay will be evaluated using the form below.*

	Point Value	Points Earned
Effective use of documents— *uses at least 5 documents*	15	_____
Accuracy— *includes correct information*	15	_____
Depth and detail— *supports main ideas with facts*	10	_____
Knowledge of social studies— *uses information beyond supplied documents*	10	_____
Clarity/Organization— *clearly expresses and logically develops ideas*	10	_____
Language mechanics— *uses proper spelling, grammar, and style*	10	_____
Correct format— *includes introduction, supporting paragraphs, and conclusion*	10	_____
TOTAL	**80**	_____

Comments: _____

_____

_____

Part A Score _____   Part B Score _____   **TOTAL SCORE** _____

10

DBQ THEME:
THE GROWTH OF INDUSTRY

DIRECTIONS:

This task is based on the accompanying documents (1–9). Some of these documents have been edited to help you with the task. The essay is designed to test your ability to work with historical documents and your knowledge of the growth of industry in America. Carefully analyze the documents as you complete **Part A**. Your responses should help you to write the essay in **Part B**.

HISTORICAL CONTEXT:

In the late nineteenth and early twentieth centuries, American industry boomed. "Captains of Industry" created large and powerful companies, which transformed the American economy and had a tremendous impact on American society. The workers who fueled this growing economy were faced with increasingly difficult and dangerous work, long hours, and little pay.

TASK:

- Describe at least two positive developments that were a result of American industrial growth in the late nineteenth and early twentieth centuries.

- Describe at least two negative developments that were a result of American industrial growth in the late nineteenth and early twentieth centuries.

PART A—SHORT-ANSWER SECTION

The following documents relate to the industrial growth in America. Examine each document carefully and answer the questions that follow.

Document 1: Andrew Carnegie—*Wealth* (1889)

In the past, goods were manufactured in the home, or in small workshops which formed part of the household. The employer and his apprentices worked side by side, the workers living with their employer, and therefore subject to the same conditions. When these apprentices rose to be masters, there was little or no change in their way of life, and they, in turn, educated succeeding apprentices in the same routine.

The result of such a means of manufacture was crude items at high prices. Today the world obtains goods of excellent quality at prices, which even the last generation would have thought unbelievable. The poor enjoy what the rich could not before afford. What were the luxuries have become the necessaries of life. The laborer has now more comforts than the farmer had a few generations ago. The farmer has more luxuries than the landlord once had, and is more richly dressed and better housed. The landlord has books and pictures rarer and artwork more splendid than a king could then obtain.

The price we pay for this change is, no doubt, great. We assemble thousands of workers in the factory, and in the mine, of whom the employer can know little or nothing; and to whom he is little better than a myth. All exchange between them is at an end. Under the law of competition, the employer of thousands is forced to be very economical, among which the wages paid to workers figures largely, and often there is friction between the employer and the employed.

1. According to Carnegie, what are two ways in which Americans benefit from changes in manufacturing?

_____

_____

_____(2)

2. What are two ways that the relationship between employers and workers changed, according to this

article? _____

_____

_____(2)

May be copied for classroom use. *Teaching and Using Document-Based Questions for Middle School* by Edward O'Connor (Portsmouth, NH: Teacher Ideas Press); ©2004.

Document 2: Wealth's Influence on Government (1883)

Great collections of wealth, whether individual or corporate, tend to corrupt government and take it out of the control of the masses of the people. "Nothing is more fearful than a million dollars—except two million dollars." Great wealth always supports the party in power, no matter how corrupt it may be. It never supports reform, for it instinctively fears change. It never struggles against misgovernment. When threatened by the holders of political power it does not protest, nor appeal to the people; it buys them off. It is in this way, no less than by its direct interference, that great wealth corrupts government, and helps to make politics a trade.

1. What are two ways that wealth influences government, according to this article?

_____

_____

_____

_____

_____(2)

Document 3: The Rise in Labor Unions

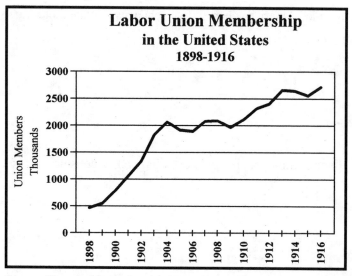

1. Approximately how much did labor union membership increase between 1898 and 1916?

_____

_____

_____

_____(1)

Source: Historical Statistics of the United States

Document 4: A Visit to the Steel Mills at Homestead, Pa. (1894)

"It's a dog's life," said my guide. "Now these men work twelve hours, and sleep and eat ten more. You can see a man don't have much time for anything else. You can't see your friends, or do anything but work."

Upon such toil rests the splendor of American civilization . . .

"The men call this the death trap," said my guide, as we stood in the edge of the building; "They wipe a man out of there every little while." "In what way does death come?" I asked. "Oh, all kinds of ways. Sometimes a chain breaks and a ladle tips over, and the iron explodes, sometimes the slag falls on the workmen from that roadway up there. Of course, if everything is working all smooth and a man watches out, why, all right! But you take it after they've been on duty twelve hours without sleep, and running like crazy, everybody tired and groggy, and it's a different story." My guide went on: "You take it back at the beam mill—you saw how the men have to scatter when the carriers or the cranes move—well, sometimes they don't get out of the way, the men who should give warning don't do it quick enough."

"What do these men get who are shoveling slag up there?"

"Fourteen cents an hour."

"So a man works in peril of his life for fourteen cents an hour?"

"That's what he does. It ain't the only business he does it in, either."

1. Name two dangers faced by workers in the steel mill, according to this article.

_____

_____

_____(2)

2. Besides physical danger, name two other features of work in the steel mill that were unpleasant or

unfair. _____

_____

_____

_____(2)

Document 5: Photograph of a Georgia Cotton Mill (1909)

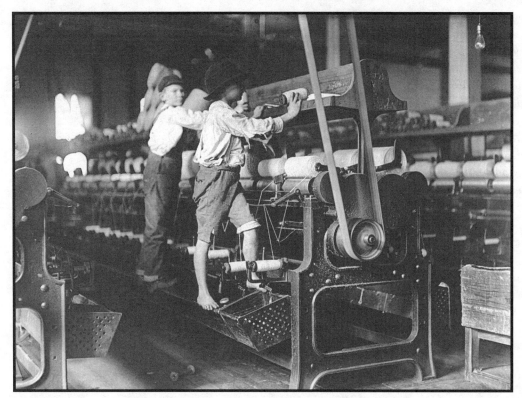

Courtesy National Archives

Bibb Mill No. 1, Macon, GA. Many youngsters [worked] here. Some boys and girls were so small, they had to climb up onto the spinning frame to mend broken threads and to put back the empty bobbins.

1. What are the workers doing in this photograph?

_____

_____

_____(1)

2. What social problem is shown in this photograph?

_____

_____

_____(1)

Document 6: Women at Work

One major change at the turn of the twentieth century was that more and more women were working outside the home. By 1910, there were more than seven million women in the workforce, more than triple the number working in the 1870s. This change sparked a great deal of argument over the role of women in society. Below is but one of many different points of view on the subject.

With the freedom of industrial opportunity has come that greatest of blessings, the freedom of choice in marriage. Under the old way, the poor girl married because she had to be taken care of; the rich girl because her life was without aim or occupation and was considered by herself and everybody else a failure until she secured a husband. The necessity was practically the same in both cases. Now the one is enabled to take care of herself, and the other is permitted to follow whatever pursuit she finds makes her the most happy. And while each expects to marry, each intends to wait until the husband comes whom she can love, respect and honor until "death do they part." Under no other conditions should any woman marry.

1. According to this article, why is there less pressure for modern women to find a husband?

_____

_____

_____

_____

_____(1)

Document 7: The Memoirs of John D. Rockefeller (1909)

For years the Standard Oil Company has developed step by step, and I am convinced that it has done well its work of supplying to the people the products from petroleum at prices which have decreased as the efficiency of the business has been built up. It gradually extended its services first to the large cities, and then to towns, and now to the smallest places, going to the homes of its customers, delivering the oil to suit the convenience of the actual users. This same system is being followed out in various parts of the world. The Company has, for example, three thousand tank wagons supplying American oil to towns and even small villages in Europe. Its own depots and employees deliver it in a similar way in Japan, China, India and the chief countries of the world. Do you think this trade has been developed by anything but hard work?

This plan of selling our products direct to the consumer and the remarkably rapid growth of the business may have angered some people, which I suppose could not have been avoided. But this same idea of dealing with the customer directly has been followed by others in many lines of trade, without creating, so far as I can tell, any serious opposition.

Every week in the year for many, many years, this business has brought in to this country more than a million dollars gold, all from the products produced by American labor. I am proud of my record, and believe most Americans will be when they understand some things better.

1. What is the name of John D. Rockefeller's company?

_____

_____

_____(1)

2. According to Rockefeller, what are two ways that Americans have benefited from the business

practices of his company? _____

_____

_____

_____

_____(2)

Document 8: Description of a Coal Mine (1894)

In wet mines, gruesome fungi grow upon the wooden props that support the uncertain looking ceiling. The walls are dripping and dank. Upon them, too, frequently grows a moss-like fungus, white as a wizard's beard, that thrives in these deep places, but shrivels and dies at contact with sunlight.

Great and strangely dreadful is the earth from a mine's depth. Man is in the restless grasp of nature. It has only to tighten a little, and he is crushed like a bug. His loudest cries of agony would be as weak as his final moan to bring help from that fair land that lies, like Heaven, over his head. There is a deadly, silent enemy in the gas. If the huge fanwheel on the top of the earth should stop for a brief second, there is certain death. If a man escapes the gas, the floods, the "squeezes" of falling rock, the cars shooting through little tunnels, the dangerous elevators, the hundred perils, there usually comes to him an attack of "miner's asthma" that slowly racks and shakes him into the grave. Meanwhile he gets three dollars a day.

1. Name two dangers faced by coal miners in the nineteenth century.

_____

_____

_____

_____(2)

Document 9: Steel Production at the End of the Nineteenth Century

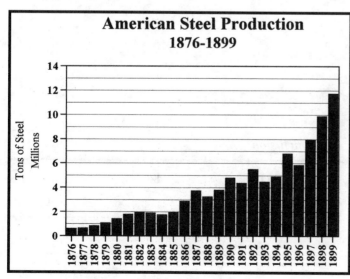

1. What can be said about the overall trend in steel production in the United States at the end of the nineteenth century?

_____

_____

_____

_____(1)

Source: Historical Statistics of the United States

PART B—ESSAY: THE GROWTH OF INDUSRY

TASK:

Using the documents in your packet, your answers to the questions in Part A, and your knowledge of social studies, write a well-developed essay that includes an introduction, supporting paragraphs, and a conclusion in which you thoroughly address the following:

- Describe at least two positive developments that were a result of American industrial growth in the late nineteenth and early twentieth centuries.
- Describe at least two negative developments that were a result of American industrial growth in the late nineteenth and early twentieth centuries.

NOTE: *your essay will be evaluated using the form below.*

	Point Value	Points Earned
Effective use of documents— *uses at least **5** documents*	15	_____
Accuracy— *includes correct information*	15	_____
Depth and detail— *supports main ideas with facts*	10	_____
Knowledge of social studies— *uses information beyond supplied documents*	10	_____
Clarity/Organization— *clearly expresses and logically develops ideas*	10	_____
Language mechanics— *uses proper spelling, grammar, and style*	10	_____
Correct format— *includes introduction, supporting paragraphs, and conclusion*	10	_____
TOTAL	**80**	_____

Comments: _____

_____

_____

Part A Score _____   Part B Score _____   **TOTAL SCORE** _____

11

DBQ Theme: The Progressive Era

DIRECTIONS:

This task is based on the accompanying documents (1–8). Some of these documents have been edited to help you with the task. The essay is designed to test your ability to work with historical documents and your knowledge of the Progressive Era. Carefully analyze the documents as you complete **Part A**. Your responses should help you to write the essay in **Part B**.

HISTORICAL CONTEXT:

A staggering number of changes occurred in the late nineteenth and early twentieth centuries: railroads stretched from coast to coast, the American frontier disappeared, immigration soared, cities swelled, and industry thrived. With these many changes came problems, and many people demanded that the government change with the times and solve these problems. During the Progressive Era, the government responded to this call. Some progressive changes resulted in more rights for American citizens, while others expanded the power of the federal government.

TASK:

- Describe two changes that occurred during the Progressive Era that directly benefited American citizens.
- Describe two changes that occurred during the Progressive Era that increased the power of the federal government.

PART A—SHORT-ANSWER SECTION

The following documents relate to the Progressive Era. Examine each document carefully, and answer the questions that follow.

Document 1: Passages from *The History of the Standard Oil Company* (1904)

> *Mr. Rockefeller was going to have things his own way, for who was there to stop him, to dispute his position? No one, except that back in northwestern Pennsylvania, in scrubby little oil towns, in dingy shanties, by rusty, deserted oil stills, men still talked about how unfair the railroad rebates were, the injustice of restraint of trade, the dangers of monopoly.*
>
> *Rockefeller has for forty years bent all the power of his great abilities to creating and carrying out a system of illegal and unjust practices by common railroad carriers. He has done more than any other person to fasten on this country the most serious interference which today the whole country is struggling in vain to get rid of. Our national life is in every way much poorer, uglier, and meaner for the kind of influence he has . . .*

1. Name two of John D. Rockefeller's business practices that were unfair, according to the author.

_____

_____

_____

_____

_____(2)

2. According to the author, what are two ways in which Rockefeller affected life in America?

_____

_____

_____

_____

_____(2)

May be copied for classroom use. *Teaching and Using Document-Based Questions for Middle School* by Edward O'Connor (Portsmouth, NH: Teacher Ideas Press); ©2004.

Document 2: *The Jungle* by Upton Sinclair (1906)

There was never the least attention paid to what was cut up for sausage. There would be meat that had tumbled out on the floor, in the dirt and saw-dust, where the workers had tramped and spit uncounted billions of germs. There would be meat stored in great piles in rooms, and water from leaky roofs would drip over it, and thousands of rats would race about on it. It was too dark in these storage places to see well, but a man could run his hand over these piles of meat and sweep off handfuls of the dried dung of rats. These rats were nuisances, and the packers would put poisoned bread out for them; they would die and then the rats, bread and meat would go into the hoppers together. This is no fairy story, and no joke. There were things that went into the sausage in comparison with which a poisoned rat was a tidbit.

1. Name two things that happened in the meat packing industry that were unhealthy.

_____

_____

_____(2)

Document 3: Theodore Roosevelt Proposes a Law (1905)

I recommend that a law be enacted to regulate interstate commerce in misla-beled and impure foods, drinks, and drugs. Such a law would protect the proper manufacture and trade, and would secure the health and welfare of the consuming public. The sale of food-stuffs which have been contaminated or polluted so as to injure health or to deceive purchasers should be forbidden.

1. What practice did Roosevelt want Congress to make illegal?

_____

_____

_____(1)

2. How would this law benefit the American people?

_____

_____

_____(1)

Document 4: Laws of the Progressive Era

SOME FEDERAL LAWS OF THE PROGRESSIVE ERA		
LAW	YEAR	DESCRIPTION
Elkins Act	1903	Outlawed railroad rebates, so railroads couldn't offer special deals to wealthy clients
Hepburn Act	1906	Allowed the government to set railroad rates through the Interstate Commerce Commission
Pure Food and Drug Act	1906	Required manufacturers to list ingredients of food products and outlawed false advertising.
Publicity Act	1910	Required politicians to make campaign contributions public
Clayton Anti-Trust Act	1914	Strengthened the Sherman Anti-Trust Act, making anti-competitive practices in business illegal

1. Name two steps the government took during the Progressive Era to control unfair business practices.

_____

_____

_____

_____

_____(2)

2. Which law might make it harder for businesses to influence politicians?

_____

_____

_____

_____(1)

Document 5: Headlines from the *New York Times*

May 16, 1911

STANDARD OIL COMPANY MUST DISSOLVE IN 6 MONTHS;
ONLY UNREASONABLE RESTRAINT OF TRADE FORBIDDEN
AND OF SUCH UNREASONABLE RESTRAINT THE SUPREME COURT
FINDS THE STANDARD GUILTY

MAY 30, 1911

TOBACCO TRUST FOUND GUILTY AND MUST DISSOLVE;
COURT IS TO FIX LEGAL FORM OF BIG BUSINESS
SUPREME COURT HOLDS ALL THE DEFENDANTS GUILTY
OF VIOLATING THE SHERMAN ACT

1. Which two companies were found guilty of breaking the Sherman Antitrust Act?

_____

_____

_____

_____

_____(2)

2. What was the penalty for these companies when they were found guilty?

_____

_____

_____

_____(1)

Document 6: Meat Inspection Act (1906)

Meat and meat food products are an important source of the Nation's total supply of food. They are consumed throughout the nation and it is essential in the public interest that the health and welfare of consumers be protected by assuring that meat and meat food products distributed to them are wholesome, so as not to contain poisonous or harmful substances, and are properly marked, labeled and packaged. Unwholesome and mislabeled meat and meat food products are injurious to the public welfare and cause injury to consumers.

1. According to this law, what are two reasons why it is important for the government to make sure

meat products are healthy? _____

_____

_____

_____

_____(2)

2. According to this document, what will the inspection of the meat industry prevent?

_____

_____

_____

_____(1)

Document 7: Two Progressive Amendments

SIXTEENTH AMENDMENT
Ratified April 3, 1913

*The Congress shall have power to lay and collect taxes on incomes,
from whatever source derived . . .*

SEVENTEENTH AMENDMENT
Ratified on April 8, 1913

*The Senate of the United States shall be composed of two Senators
from each state, elected by the people thereof . . .*

1. What power was given to the Federal government in the Sixteenth Amendment?

_____

_____

_____

_____

_____(1)

2. What power was given to the American people in the Seventeenth Amendment?

_____

_____

_____

_____

_____(1)

Document 8: Women's Suffrage in New York State (1917)

Courtesy Library of Congress

Before the ratification of the Nineteenth Amendment in 1920, women were allowed to vote in several states. Here, women from New York vote for the first time in 1917.

1. What right did women gain during the Progressive Era?

_____

_____

_____

_____

_____(1)

PART B—ESSAY: THE PROGRESSIVE ERA

TASK:

Using the documents in your packet, your answers to the questions in Part A, and your knowledge of social studies, write a well-developed essay that includes an introduction, supporting paragraphs, and a conclusion in which you thoroughly address the following:

- Describe two changes that occurred during the Progressive Era that directly benefited American citizens.
- Describe two changes that occurred during the Progressive Era that increased the power of the Federal government.

NOTE: *your essay will be evaluated using the form below.*

	Point Value	Points Earned
Effective use of documents— *uses at least 5 documents*	15	_____
Accuracy— *includes correct information*	15	_____
Depth and detail— *supports main ideas with facts*	10	_____
Knowledge of social studies— *uses information beyond supplied documents*	10	_____
Clarity/Organization— *clearly expresses and logically develops ideas*	10	_____
Language mechanics— *uses proper spelling, grammar, and style*	10	_____
Correct format— *includes introduction, supporting paragraphs, and conclusion*	10	_____
TOTAL	**80**	_____

Comments: _____

_____

_____

Part A Score _____   Part B Score _____   **TOTAL SCORE** _____

12

⬤

DBQ THEME: AMERICA IN THE 1920S

DIRECTIONS:

This task is based on the accompanying documents (1–9). Some of these documents have been edited to help you with the task. The essay is designed to test your ability to work with historical documents and your knowledge of the 1920s. Carefully analyze the documents as you complete **Part A**. Your responses should help you to write the essay in **Part B**.

HISTORICAL CONTEXT:

Many people living in the 1920s felt that they were living in an exciting time. They called it the "Roaring Twenties"; sometimes it was even referred to as the "Modern Decade." In many ways it was just that. Flush with their successes in World War I, Americans looked forward to a carefree time of "normalcy," freedom, and prosperity. Many changes were taking place in American society, the economy was thriving, and America was at peace. However, not all Americans were able to enjoy these times. For all the exciting events and features of the 1920s, there were many problems that haunted American society. Historians and students need to look carefully at this decade and decide: Were the Twenties an exciting and modern decade? Or were they a time of troubles?

TASK:

- Describe at least two features of the 1920s that made them a positive, exciting time in American history.

- Describe at least two social problems faced by Americans in the 1920s.

PART A—SHORT-ANSWER SECTION

The following documents relate to the 1920s. Examine each document carefully and answer the questions that follow.

Document 1: *Life* Magazine Cover (1926)

Courtesy Library of Congress

To many people, this cover of *Life* shows what the "Roaring Twenties" were all about.

1. What are two things about this illustration that suggest the 1920s were a time of prosperity?

_____

_____

_____(2)

May be copied for classroom use. *Teaching and Using Document-Based Questions for Middle School* by Edward O'Connor (Portsmouth, NH: Teacher Ideas Press); ©2004.

Document 2: A Poem by Langston Hughes (1925)

Poet Langston Hughes is remembered as one of the most important influences of the Harlem Renaissance.

I, Too, Sing America

I, too, sing America
I am the darker brother
They send me to eat in the kitchen
When company comes.
But I laugh,
And eat well,
And grow strong.
Tomorrow
I'll sit at the table
When company comes
Nobody'll dare
Say to me,
'Eat in the kitchen'
Then.
Besides, they'll see how
Beautiful I am
And be ashamed—
I, too, am America.

1. What does this poem suggest about the way African Americans were treated in the 1920s?

_____

_____

_____

_____(1)

2. What message of hope did Hughes give to African Americans in this poem?

_____

_____

_____

_____(1)

This page may not be reproduced for any purpose.

Document 3: Statement by Bartolomeo Vanzetti (1927)

In 1921 Nicola Sacco and Bartolomeo Vanzetti were convicted for killing two men during a robbery outside of Boston. Their case became the subject of nationwide attention as there was very little direct evidence against them. A great deal of time during their trial, however, was spent on the immigrants' radical political beliefs. Sacco and Vanzetti were executed on August 23, 1927. The following is taken from Vanzetti's last statement in court.

We were tried during a time that has now passed into history. I mean that, a time when there was hysterical resentment and hate against the people of our principles, against the foreigner, and it seems to me that the court has done all that was in its power to do, to stir up the emotions of the jury, to prejudice the jury against us.

Well, I have already said that I am not only not guilty of these crimes, but that I have never committed a crime in my life—I never steal, and I have never spilled blood. But my belief is that I have suffered for things that I am guilty of. I have suffered because I am radical and I am a radical; I have suffered because I am Italian and indeed I am Italian. I am so convinced to be right that if you could execute me two times, I would live again to do what I have done already. I have finished. Thank you.

1. Why did Vanzetti feel that he did not get a fair trial?

_____

_____

_____

_____

_____(1)

2. According to Vanzetti, what are two reasons why he has suffered?

_____

_____

_____

_____

_____(2)

Document 4: A Criticism of Prohibition (1926)

After six years of national prohibition, and the spending of vast sums of money to enforce the law, the manufacture of alcoholic beverages has become a great and growing industry. The money value of the output of these products was estimated as several times as great as the total amount spent on whiskey, wine, beer and other alcoholic beverages before the ratification of the Eighteenth Amendment.

Prohibition has created a vast army of rum-runners, moonshiners, bootleggers, and corrupt public officials, breeding a condition of lawlessness unequaled in the history of the Republic. The cost of even moderately effective control of the trade would amount to great sums, being estimated that it would require at least $75,000,000 a year to restrain the sale of alcohol in New York State alone.

1. According to the selection above, how much would it cost to enforce Prohibition?

_____

_____

_____

_____

_____(1)

2. According to the author, what are two other problems that developed because of Prohibition?

_____

_____

_____

_____

_____(2)

Document 5: Swimsuits of the 20s

Courtesy the Denver Public Library

There were many changes in fashion during the 1920s, and swimwear was no exception. Some of the suits worn by these women may have caused a stir in their day, since many people still considered it inappropriate for a woman to show bare legs in public.

1. Describe the differences between some of the bathing suits in this photograph.

_____

_____

_____(1)

2. How are these bathing suits different from suits today?

_____

_____

_____

_____(1)

Document 6: A Declaration of the Ku Klux Klan (1922)

We solemnly declare to all mankind: that the Knights of the Ku Klux Klan, incorporated, is the original Ku Klux Klan organized in the year 1866, and active during the Reconstruction period of American history and by and under its name is revived, remodeled and expanded into a fraternal, patriotic society of national scope.

We invite all men who can qualify to become citizens of the Invisible Empire to approach our domain, join us in our noble work of expanding our boundaries and sharing the gospel of "Klancraft", to share with us the glory of performing the sacred duty of protecting womanhood, to maintain forever the God-given supremacy of the white race, to remember the noble achievements of our fathers, and to safeguard the sacred rights, privileges and institutions of our government.

1. According to this document, when was the Ku Klux Klan first organized?

_____

_____

_____

_____

_____(1)

2. What are two of the most important duties of the Klan, according to this declaration?

_____

_____

_____

_____(2)

Document 7: The Candidacy of Al Smith

Religion became a major issue in the 1928 presidential election between Herbert Hoover and Al Smith. Smith was the first major presidential candidate who was a member of the Catholic Church, and this was a major criticism of his campaign. The issue became intensified when a man named Charles C. Marshall published a letter in *The Atlantic Monthly* in which he claimed Smith was not fit to be president because of his religious beliefs. Here, Smith, four-time governor of New York State, looks back on this campaign in his autobiography.

> *The appearance in the public prints of the Marshall letter was a warning of what would have to be dealt with later and what would undoubtedly become a campaign issue, if I were nominated for president. The Marshall letter came as something of a shock to thoughtful people throughout the country. Here was the first time in our history that the qualifications of a man for public office were openly challenged because he had a particular religious belief. Small fry politicians may have used such tactics under cover, but the Marshall letter brought the religious question into the open, printed as it was in one of the most reputable magazines in the country.*

1. According to Smith, why did the Marshall letter come as such a shock to some people?

_____

_____

_____

_____(1)

Document 8: Anti-Lynching Advertisement (1922)

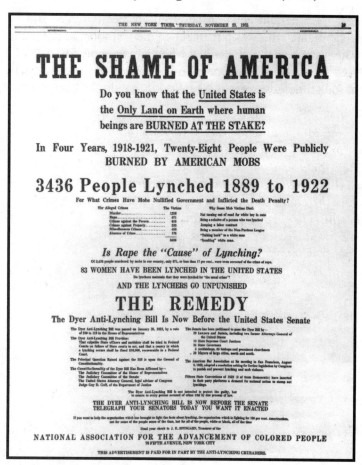

Courtesy The New York Times

Since the end of the Civil War, African Americans were often subjected to mob violence. This ad was published in 1922 in support of an anti-lynching bill. The bill passed in the House of Representatives, but was defeated in the Senate.

1. According to this advertisement, what was the "Shame of America"?

_____

_____(1)

2. What did this advertisement urge people to do?

_____

_____

_____(1)

Document 9: Line Graphs—Automobiles and Radios

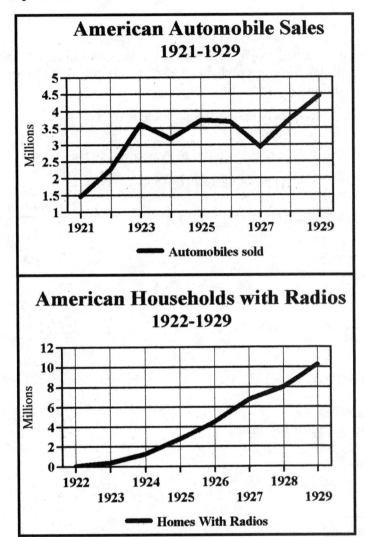

Source: Historical Statistics of the United States

1. Which of the two products charted above increased most steadily?

_____

_____(1)

2. About how many more cars were sold in 1929 than in 1921?

_____

_____(1)

PART B—ESSAY: AMERICA IN THE 1920s

TASK:

Using the documents in your packet, your answers to the questions in Part A, and your knowledge of social studies, write a well-developed essay that includes an introduction, supporting paragraphs, and a conclusion in which you thoroughly address the following:

- Describe at least two features of the 1920s that made them a positive, exciting time in American history.
- Describe at least two social problems faced by Americans in the 1920s.

NOTE: *your essay will be evaluated using the form below.*

	Point Value	Points Earned
Effective use of documents— *uses at least 5 documents*	15	_____
Accuracy— *includes correct information*	15	_____
Depth and detail— *supports main ideas with facts*	10	_____
Knowledge of social studies— *uses information beyond supplied documents*	10	_____
Clarity/Organization— *clearly expresses and logically develops ideas*	10	_____
Language mechanics— *uses proper spelling, grammar, and style*	10	_____
Correct format— *includes introduction, supporting paragraphs, and conclusion*	10	_____
TOTAL	**80**	_____

Comments: _____

_____

_____

Part A Score _____   Part B Score _____   **TOTAL SCORE** _____

13

DBQ THEME: THE GREAT DEPRESSION AND THE NEW DEAL

DIRECTIONS:

This task is based on the accompanying documents (1–8). Some of these documents have been edited to help you with the task. The essay is designed to test your ability to work with historical documents and your knowledge of the Great Depression and the New Deal. Carefully analyze the documents as you complete **Part A**. Your responses should help you to write the essay in **Part B**.

HISTORICAL CONTEXT:

The Great Depression was a time of crisis for the American people. Many people lost their jobs, their savings, or both. Businesses failed, and farmers struggled. When Franklin D. Roosevelt swept into the presidency in 1932, he promised to take action—a promise he made good on very quickly. During his administration, the government began a series of programs that became known as the New Deal. These programs together sought to achieve three goals: relief, recovery, and reform. Even though many people welcomed the New Deal as an attempt to solve a major national problem, others complained about the changes it brought about, or that it didn't go far enough.

TASK:

- Discuss at least one success of the New Deal.
- Discuss at least one failure of the New Deal.
- Describe at least two lasting changes brought on by the New Deal.

PART A—SHORT-ANSWER SECTION

The following documents relate to the Great Depression and the New Deal. Examine each document carefully and answer the questions that follow.

Document 1: Chart—Some New Deal Programs

A Sample of the "Alphabet Agencies" of the New Deal			
Act or Agency	Year	Purpose	Role
Agricultural Adjustment Act (AAA)	1933	Recovery	Helped farmers by paying them to produce less, therefore driving farm prices higher.
Civilian Conservation Corps (CCC)	1933	Relief	Created jobs for young men in areas of forestry, conservation, and construction of recreation areas.
Federal Emergency Relief Act (FERA)	1933	Relief	Gave out millions of dollars of relief to the unemployed.
Federal Deposit Insurance Corporation (FDIC)	1933	Reform	Insures deposits in savings accounts so individuals need not worry about bank failures.
Public Works Administration	1933	Relief and Recovery	Created jobs in construction of highways, bridges, buildings and other public works projects
Securities and Exchange Commission	1934	Reform	This agency was created to protect investors from unfair practices in the stock market.
Works Progress Administration (WPA)	1935	Relief	Created jobs for people in a wide variety of areas including: artists, actors, writers, builders, etc....

1. List two New Deal programs that created jobs.

_____

_____

_____(2)

2. Name two groups of people that were helped by New Deal programs.

_____

_____

_____(2)

May be copied for classroom use. *Teaching and Using Document-Based Questions for Middle School* by Edward O'Connor (Portsmouth, NH: Teacher Ideas Press); ©2004.

Document 2: Oral History: Gardiner C. Means

The NRA (National Recovery Administration) was one of the most successful things the New Deal did. It ended when it should have ended. But when it was created, American business had completely lost its spirit. Violent price cutting and wage cutting ... nobody could make any plans for tomorrow. Everybody was going around in circles. The NRA changed the attitudes of business and the public. It revived the belief that something could be done.

Most important, the Nineteenth Century idea that government should leave business alone was ended. The government had a role to play in industrial activity. In the two years of the NRA, industrial production went up remarkably.

Gardiner C. Means worked in several areas in the federal government during the 1930s and 40s, including the U.S. Department of Agriculture and the NRA.

1. What are two reasons the NRA was successful, according to Mr. Means?

_____

_____

_____

_____

_____(2)

2. What major change occurred as a result of the NRA, according to this passage?

_____

_____

_____

_____(1)

Document 3: A Letter to FDR in Response to a "Fireside Chat" (1934)

Dear Mr. President,

For the first time in my life, I am writing to a public official. For the first time in my life, I feel like I have a president. I read what you write. I listen to what you say. I believe in you.

You asked us tonight to take stock of our own affairs. Yes, I am better off. My brother, who was out of work for over three years, got a job last January, and I no longer have to contribute to his support. I do not earn more money, but have a feeling of greater security in my position. But better than the economic side is my feeling of pride and satisfaction in you as my President. For the first time I feel that the leader of my country has some interest in me— that those in my walk of life are not altogether forgotten.

I am convinced that your program is sincere and we Americans recognize and appreciate this rare trait. It's what we want. Not perfection, nor miracles, but a square deal.

Sincerely,

Alice Timoney
New York City, New York

1. Give two reasons Ms. Timoney supports President Roosevelt.

_____

_____

_____

_____

_____(2)

Document 4: The Civilian Conservation Corps at Work (1933)

Courtesy the F.D.R. Library

The CCC employed millions of people nationwide. Here, a crew of young men works on a highway beautification project.

1. Describe the kind of work the men in this photograph are doing.

_____

_____(1)

2. How did these men benefit from the New Deal?

_____

_____(1)

Document 5: A 1960 Interview with George Bigge, Member of the Social Security Board 1937–1946

We are so accustomed to having the Government—and when we say government now we mean Federal Government—trying to solve our social and economic problems that it's difficult to realize how different things were before the New Deal. The Social Security program is just one illustration of that difference and serves as a good example. Just one of the programs established under the Social Security Act, Old Age and Survivors Insurance, is today paying out 50 percent more money regularly than the entire Federal budget was at the time the Act was created.

Before the New Deal, people didn't think too much about asking the Government to do anything about their problems. The pressure didn't really come until the depression of the 30's when unemployment reached 30 and 35 percent. In my state, Rhode Island, in 1933, 36 percent of the working force was unemployed, and in Michigan it was 45 percent. It was that critical situation which brought about a rethinking of our whole attitude toward the Government's relationship to the individual's need, particularly the Federal Government.

1. According to this interview, what are two changes that were a result of the New Deal?

_____

_____

_____

_____

_____(2)

Document 6: Oral History—David Kennedy

1937 and 1939 were interesting periods. We hadn't come out of the Depression. It was deep-set.

We really had not made a substantial recovery from the deep Depression of the early Thirties. Unemployment was still very high. The New Deal programs were not stimulating the way people thought. There was a sort of a defeated attitude—that the government just had to do all this for the people. It was not until the war, with its economic thrust, that we pulled out of it. The war got us out of it, not the New Deal policies.

The New Deal took care of immediate suffering in part of the areas. I'm not criticizing it in that sense. But it didn't pull the thing up so that private business could take its place and replace it. Roosevelt gave us quite a bit of hope early. He probably saved us from complete collapse, in that sense.

David Kennedy was on the Federal Reserve Board in the 1930s, and later served as Secretary of the Treasury under President Nixon.

1. According to Kennedy, what ended the Great Depression?

_____

_____

_____

_____

_____(1)

2. According to this passage, what are two accomplishments of the New Deal?

_____

_____

_____

_____

_____(2)

Document 7: Line Graph—Unemployment

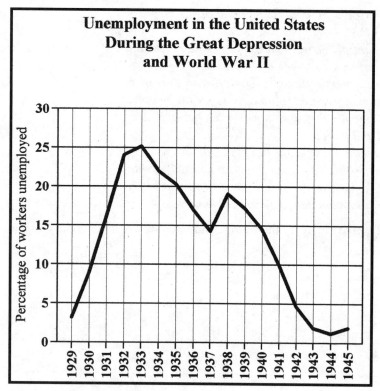

Source: Historical Statistics of the United States

The Great Depression began in 1929 with the Stock Market Crash.

World War II began in Europe in 1939.

American involvement in World War II began in 1941.

1. When did unemployment reach its highest level?

_____

_____

_____

_____(1)

2. When did unemployment return to the level it was when the Great Depression began?

_____

_____

_____(1)

Document 8: Oral History—Ben Isaacs

We tried to struggle along living day by day. Then I couldn't pay the rent. I had a little car . . . I sold it for $15 in order to buy some food for the family. I had three little children. I didn't have a nickel in my pocket.

I didn't want to go on relief. Believe me, when I was forced to go to the office of the relief, the tears were running out of my eyes. I couldn't bear myself to take money from anybody for nothing. If it wasn't for those kids—I tell you the truth—many a time it came to my mind to go commit suicide than go ask for relief. But somebody has to take care of those kids . . .

I went to the relief and then, after a lotta red tape and investigation; they gave me $45 a month. Out of that $45 we had to pay rent, we had to buy food and clothing for the children. So how long can $45 go? I was paying $30 on the rent. I went and find another cheaper place for $15 a month. I'm telling you; today a dog wouldn't live in that type of place. Such a dirty, filthy, dark place.

Wherever I went to get a job, I couldn't get no job. I went around selling shoe laces and razor blades. That kept going until 1940, practically. 1939 the war started. Things start to get a little better. My wife found a job in a restaurant for $20 a week. Right away, I sent a letter to the relief people: I don't think I would need their help any more. I was disgusted with relief, so ashamed. I couldn't face it any more.

Ben Isaacs was a clothing salesman in Chicago.

1. How was Mr. Isaacs affected by the Depression?

_____

_____

_____

_____

_____(1)

2. Why was Mr. Isaacs unhappy about being on relief?

_____

_____

_____

_____(1)

PART B—ESSAY: THE GREAT DEPRESSION AND THE NEW DEAL

TASK:

Using the documents in your packet, your answers to the questions in Part A, and your knowledge of social studies, write a well-developed essay that includes an introduction, supporting paragraphs, and a conclusion in which you thoroughly address the following:

- Discuss at least one success of the New Deal.
- Discuss at least one failure of the New Deal.
- Describe at least two lasting changes brought on by the New Deal.

NOTE: *your essay will be evaluated using the form below.*

	Point Value	Points Earned
Effective use of documents— *uses at least 5 documents*	15	_____
Accuracy— *includes correct information*	15	_____
Depth and detail— *supports main ideas with facts*	10	_____
Knowledge of social studies— *uses information beyond supplied documents*	10	_____
Clarity/Organization— *clearly expresses and logically develops ideas*	10	_____
Language mechanics— *uses proper spelling, grammar, and style*	10	_____
Correct format— *includes introduction, supporting paragraphs, and conclusion*	10	_____
TOTAL	**80**	_____

Comments: _____

_____

_____

Part A Score _____   Part B Score _____   **TOTAL SCORE** _____

14

DBQ THEME:
AMERICA IN WORLD WAR II

DIRECTIONS:

This task is based on the accompanying documents (1–9). Some of these documents have been edited to help you with the task. The essay is designed to test your ability to work with historical documents and your knowledge of World War II. Carefully analyze the documents as you complete **Part A**. Your responses should help you to write the essay in **Part B**.

HISTORICAL CONTEXT:

The United States played a major role in the allied victory in World War II. Millions of brave American soldiers served their country in this conflict, with hundreds of thousands killed, and even more wounded. Although our losses were great, they seem small when compared to those of the other nations involved. Besides the courage and sacrifice of our fighting forces, perhaps America's greatest contribution to the war effort was found in its industrial strength. American workers supplied their soldiers and those of their allies with the equipment and material necessary to achieve victory.

TASK:

- Describe the role of American industry in World War II.
- Describe at least two things American citizens did to help with war production.

PART A—SHORT-ANSWER SECTION

The following documents relate to World War II. Examine each document carefully and answer the questions that follow.

Document 1: President Roosevelt's Annual Message to Congress (January 6, 1942)

> *Modern methods of warfare make it a task not only of shooting and fighting, but an even more urgent one of working and producing.*
>
> *The superiority of the United States in weapons must be overwhelming— so overwhelming that the Axis nations can never hope to catch up with it. In order to attain this overwhelming superiority the United States must build planes and tanks and guns to the utmost limit of our national capacity. We have the ability to produce arms not only for our own forces but also for the armies, navies, and air forces fighting on our side.*
>
> *This production of ours in the United States must be raised far above its present levels, even though it will mean the dislocation of the lives and occupations of millions of our own people.*
>
> *We must strain every existing weapon-producing facility to the utmost. We must convert every available factory and tool to war production. That goes all the way from the greatest plants to the smallest—from the huge automobile industry to the village machine shop.*
>
> *Production for war is based on metals and raw materials—steel, copper, rubber, aluminum, zinc, tin. Greater and greater amounts of them will have to be diverted to war purposes. Civilian use of them will have to be cut further and still further—and, in many cases, completely eliminated.*

1. According to Roosevelt, what would make the United States successful in World War II?

_____

_____

_____(1)

2. Name two changes to the American economy that Roosevelt suggests in this address.

_____

_____

_____(2)

May be copied for classroom use. *Teaching and Using Document-Based Questions for Middle School* by Edward O'Connor (Portsmouth, NH: Teacher Ideas Press); ©2004.

Document 2: Photo of a War Production Plant (1942)

Courtesy Library of Congress

1. What is being produced at this factory?

_____

_____

_____(1)

2. What does this photograph suggest about the strength of American war production?

_____

_____

_____(1)

Document 3: Scrap Drive Poster

Courtesy National Archives

1. In this poster, what material are Americans being asked to donate for the war effort?

_____

_____(1)

2. What will this material be used for?

_____

_____

_____(1)

Document 4: Lend-Lease Agreement (1942)

The President of the United States has determined, based on the Act of Congress on March 11, 1941, that the defense of the United Kingdom against aggression is vital to the defense of the United States of America, and so the United States of America has given and is continuing to give the United Kingdom aid in resisting aggression.

The Government of the United States of America will continue to supply the Government of the United Kingdom with defense articles, defense services and defense information as the President shall approve to be provided.

The Government of the United Kingdom will return to the United States of America at the end of the present emergency, such defense articles that have not been destroyed, lost, or used up.

1. According to this document, why did the United States agree to give aid to the United Kingdom?

_____

_____

_____

_____

_____(1)

2. Name two things that the United States agreed to give the United Kingdom in this agreement.

_____

_____

_____

_____

_____(2)

Document 5: Line Graph—War Production

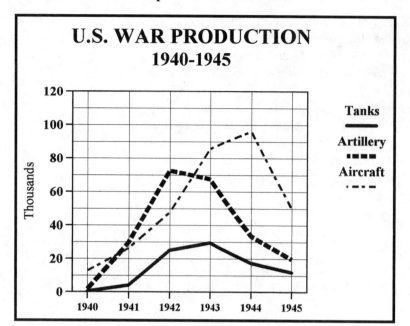

Source: Dear, I.C.B., Oxford Companion to World War II

1. How many tanks did the U.S. produce in 1943?

_____

_____

_____

_____(1)

2. What can be said about U.S. war production between 1941 and 1942?

_____

_____

_____

_____(1)

Document 6: War Bond Poster

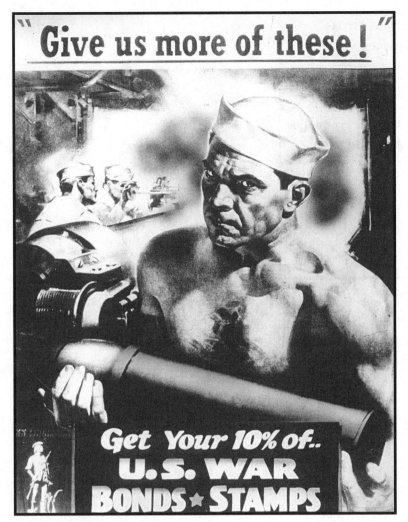

"Give us more of these!"

Get Your 10% of..
U.S. WAR
BONDS ★ STAMPS

Courtesy National Archives

Posters like these were very common during World War II. Americans were encouraged to spend ten percent of their paychecks on war bonds to support the war effort.

1. According to this poster, for what purpose will money raised from war bonds be used?

_____

_____

_____

_____(1)

Document 7: Bar Graph—Airplanes Produced and Lost

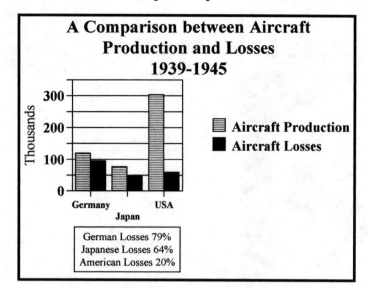

A Comparison between Aircraft Production and Losses 1939-1945

German Losses 79%
Japanese Losses 64%
American Losses 20%

Source: Gregory, Ross, Almanacs of American Life

1. Which nation lost the fewest aircraft?

_____

_____

_____

_____

_____(1)

2. Why was the United States hurt less by its losses than Germany or Japan?

_____

_____

_____

_____(1)

Document 8: Wartime Production Poster

Courtesy Library of Congress

1. What does this poster encourage workers to do?

    _____

    _____

    _____(1)

2. How did this poster include factory workers in the war effort?

    _____

    _____

    _____(1)

Document 9: World War II Statistics

HUMAN AND FINANCIAL COSTS OF WORLD WAR II

NATIONS	MILITARY DEATHS	ECONOMIC COSTS (Billions of Dollars)
UNITED STATES	292,100	350
GREAT BRITAIN	397,762	150
FRANCE	210,671	100
SOVIET UNION	7,500,000	200
GERMANY	2,850,000	300
ITALY	77,500	50
JAPAN	1,506,000	100

Source: Gregory, Almanacs

1. Which nation lost the most soldiers?

_____

_____

_____

_____

_____(1)

2. According to this chart, how did America's contribution in the war compare to that of its allies, in terms of both casualties and spending?

_____

_____

_____

_____(2)

PART B—ESSAY: AMERICA IN WORLD WAR II

TASK:

Using the documents in your packet, your answers to the questions in Part A, and your knowledge of social studies, write a well-developed essay that includes an introduction, supporting paragraphs, and a conclusion in which you thoroughly address the following:

- Describe the role of American industry in World War II.
- Describe at least two things American citizens did to help with war production.

NOTE: *your essay will be evaluated using the form below.*

	Point Value	Points Earned
Effective use of documents— *uses at least **5** documents*	15	_____
Accuracy— *includes correct information*	15	_____
Depth and detail— *supports main ideas with facts*	10	_____
Knowledge of social studies— *uses information beyond supplied documents*	10	_____
Clarity/Organization— *clearly expresses and logically develops ideas*	10	_____
Language mechanics— *uses proper spelling, grammar, and style*	10	_____
Correct format— *includes introduction, supporting paragraphs, and conclusion*	10	_____
TOTAL	**80**	_____

Comments: _____

_____

_____

_____

Part A Score _____   Part B Score _____   **TOTAL SCORE** _____

15

DBQ THEME:
AMERICA AND THE COLD WAR

DIRECTIONS:

This task is based on the accompanying documents (1–9). Some of these documents have been edited to help you with the task. The essay is designed to test your ability to work with historical documents and your knowledge of the Cold War. Carefully analyze the documents as you complete **Part A**. Your responses should help you to write the essay in **Part B**.

HISTORICAL CONTEXT:

During the Cold War, Americans viewed the Soviet Union (U.S.S.R.) with a great deal of mistrust, suspicion, and even fear. The threat of a nuclear war was always present as both nations competed for dominance. Americans believed that the Soviets were intent on spreading communism throughout the world, and some even feared the influence communists had within the United States itself. As a result, the United States government focused a great deal of its energy and resources on "fighting" the Cold War.

TASK:

- Discuss at least two ways in which the United States government reacted to the threat of communism during the Cold War.

- Identify and discuss at least two ways in which the threat of communism affected citizens of the United States.

PART A—SHORT-ANSWER SECTION

The following documents relate to the Cold War. Examine each document carefully, and answer the questions that follow.

Document 1: Assessment of the Soviet Union by American Diplomat George F. Kennan (1946)

The Soviet Union is a political force committed to the belief that there is no way to get along with the United States, and they believe it is desirable and necessary that the internal harmony of our society be disrupted, our traditional way of life be destroyed, the international power of our government be broken if Soviet power is to be secure. This is admittedly not a pleasant picture. The problem of how to cope with this force is undoubtedly the greatest task our diplomacy has ever faced and probably the greatest it will ever have to face. It should be approached with the same thoroughness and care as if it were a major strategic problem in a war . . .

1. According to Kennan, what were two goals of the Soviet Union?

_____

_____

_____

_____(2)

2. How should the United States approach problems with the Soviet Union, according to this document?

_____

_____

_____

_____(1)

May be copied for classroom use. *Teaching and Using Document-Based Questions for Middle School* by Edward O'Connor (Portsmouth, NH: Teacher Ideas Press); ©2004.

Document 2: Temporary Basement Fallout Shelter (1957)

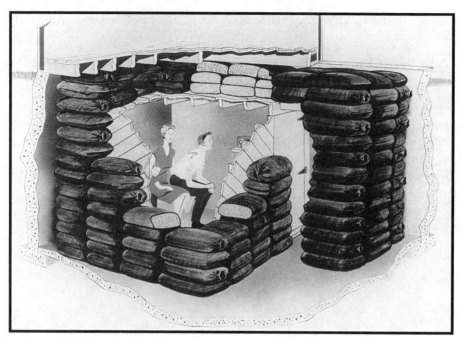

Courtesy National Archives

Shelters like the one shown above were intended to protect people from fallout from a nuclear attack. Fallout is made of radioactive particles that can cause illness and death. A typical shelter would include a stockpile of food, a battery-operated radio, flashlights, and a two-week supply of water.

1. For what purpose were fallout shelters used?

_____

_____

_____

_____(1)

2. Why did people believe these shelters were necessary?

_____

_____

_____

_____(1)

Document 3: American Reaction to Sputnik (1957)

On October 4, 1957, the Soviet Union became the first nation to launch successfully a satellite (Sputnik) into orbit around the Earth. The following passage was taken from the summary of a meeting of President Eisenhower's National Security Council on October 11, 1957.

> . . . *Secretary Herter stated that the reaction of our allies had been pretty firm and good, although even our closest allies need to be reassured that we have not been passed scientifically or militarily by the U.S.S.R. . . .*
>
> *Mr. Larson said that while we could not permit ourselves to be panicked by the Soviet achievement, he did wonder whether our plans were now satisfactory with regard to the next great breakthrough. If we lose repeatedly to the Russians as we have lost with the Earth satellite, the damage would be tremendous. We should accordingly plan, ourselves, to accomplish some of the next great breakthroughs first—for example, the achievement of a manned satellite, or getting to the moon.*

1. Why were some of America's allies concerned about the launch of Sputnik?

_____

_____

_____

_____

_____(1)

2. What did Mr. Larson suggest America should do in response to Sputnik?

_____

_____

_____

_____(1)

Document 4: Military Training in the Cold War (1952)

Courtesy National Archives

U.S. military personnel trained for the possibility of fighting in a nuclear war. Here, U.S. Marines conduct maneuvers just seconds after an atomic explosion.

1. Why are these soldiers so close to an atomic blast?

_____

_____(1)

2. What dangers did these soldiers face in participating in this type of training?

_____

_____(1)

Document 5: A Statement to the House Un-American Activities Committee (1947)

Between 1938 and 1970 the House of Representatives created a committee to investigate groups and individuals it considered dangerous and Un-American. In 1947, the "Un-American Activities Committee" investigated the motion picture industry, claiming that communist writers and actors were attempting to influence the American people through movies. A group of ten writers and directors refused to answer the question "Are you a member of the Communist Party?" and were charged with contempt of Congress, fined, and jailed. Many found it difficult to find work for years. The following is an excerpt from a statement of one of these writers, John Howard Lawson.

For a week, the House Committee on Un-American Activities has conducted an illegal and indecent trial of American citizens, whom the committee has selected to be publicly humiliated and smeared . . .

. . . The committee is trying to destroy me personally and professionally, to deprive me of my livelihood and what is dearer to me—my honor as an American. . . . The Committee has tried to justify its investigation into the thought and conscience of individuals on the grounds that these individuals put communist and un-American lines or scenes in motion pictures. When I am hired to write a motion picture, my whole purpose is to make it entertaining. . . . I don't 'sneak ideas' into movies. I never agree to make a movie unless I am sure that it serves democracy and the interests of the American people. I will never permit what I write and think to be censored by the Un-American Activities Committee.

1. Why was the House Committee on Un-American Activities investigating Mr. Lawson?

_____

_____

_____

_____

_____(1)

2. Name at least one of Lawson's main complaints about the Committee.

_____

_____

_____

_____(1)

Document 6: Soviet News Service Report on the U-2 Spy Plane Incident (1960)

On May 1, 1960, a U-2 spy plane flown by Francis Gary Powers was shot down over Soviet territory. Powers was captured and put on trial for spying, a crime for which he could be executed. Powers was later returned to the U.S. in an exchange for a Soviet spy held by the United States.

> *"As U.S. President Eisenhower has stated, flying American planes over the territory of the U.S.S.R. was, and remains the deliberate policy of the United States. Vice President Nixon stated that a continuous program of spying activities, or the so-called 'right to spy' is necessary to the United States.*
>
> *These statements by the highest officials of the United States reveal that the crime committed by U-2 pilot Powers was not a single, isolated case but only a link in the chain of U.S. aggressive measures which are leading to a tremendous increase in international tension and placing peace on the brink of war.*
>
> *The fact is, that when nations have nuclear weapons and the means of delivering them to targets in no time, aggressive acts such as these can lead to catastrophic consequences for all mankind."*

1. What evidence do the Soviets give in this document to show that the U-2 incident was not a single, isolated case? _____

_____

_____

_____

_____(1)

2. According to the Soviets, why was this sort of spying dangerous?

_____

_____

_____

_____

_____(1)

Document 7: "Duck and Cover" Drills

Courtesy The Detroit News

Air raid drills, such as the one shown in the photograph above, were a common experience for American children during the Cold War. Children were expected to "duck and cover" under desks or in basements during such drills.

1. Why are these children taking cover under their desks?

_____

_____

_____

_____

_____(1)

Document 8: John F. Kennedy's Television Address Regarding the Cuban Missile Crisis (1962)

Within the past week, we have gained unmistakable evidence that a series of offensive nuclear missile sites is now in preparation on the island of Cuba. The purpose of these bases can be none other than to provide a nuclear strike capability against the Western Hemisphere . . .

The characteristics of these new missile sites show two different types of installations. Several of them include medium range ballistic missiles, capable of carrying a nuclear warhead for a distance of more than 1000 miles. Each of these missiles, in short, is capable of striking Washington, D.C., the Panama Canal, Cape Canaveral, or any other city in the southeastern part of the United States, in Central America, or in the Caribbean area. Additional sites not yet completed appear to be designed for intermediate range ballistic missiles capable of traveling more than twice as far—and thus capable of striking most of the major cities in the Western Hemisphere. . . .

Nuclear weapons are so destructive and ballistic missiles are so swift, that any major increase in the possibility of their use or any sudden change in their deployment may well be regarded as a definite threat to peace. . . .

It shall be the policy of this nation to regard any nuclear missile launch from Cuba against any nation in the Western Hemisphere as an attack by the Soviet Union on the United States, requiring a full retaliatory response upon the Soviet Union.

1. Give two reasons why Kennedy considered these missiles a threat to peace.

_____

_____

_____

_____

_____(2)

2. What did Kennedy threaten to do if the missiles in Cuba were used?

_____

_____

_____

_____(1)

Document 9: The Arms Race

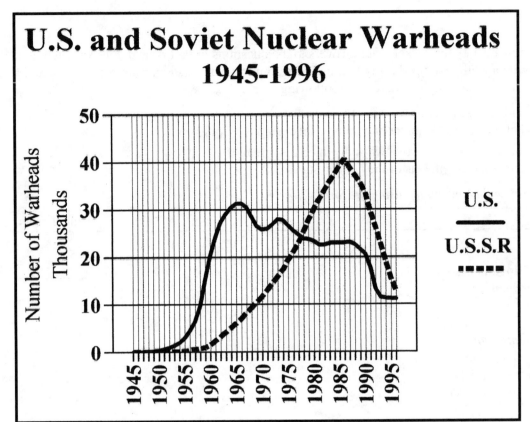

U.S. and Soviet Nuclear Warheads 1945-1996

Source: *Natural Resources Defense Council*

1. Which nation developed nuclear weapons first?

_____

_____(1)

2. Which nation developed the most nuclear weapons?

_____

_____(1)

3. Approximately how much did Soviet warheads increase between 1955 and 1985?

_____

_____(1)

PART B—ESSAY: AMERICA AND THE COLD WAR

TASK:

Using the documents in your packet, your answers to the questions in Part A, and your knowledge of social studies, write a well-developed essay that includes an introduction, supporting paragraphs, and a conclusion in which you thoroughly address the following:

- Identify and discuss at least two ways in which the United States government reacted to the threat of communism during the Cold War.
- Identify and discuss at least two ways in which the threat of communism affected citizens of the United States.

NOTE: *your essay will be evaluated using the form below.*

	Point Value	Points Earned
Effective use of documents— *uses at least* **5** *documents*	15	_____
Accuracy— *includes correct information*	15	_____
Depth and detail— *supports main ideas with facts*	10	_____
Knowledge of social studies— *uses information beyond supplied documents*	10	_____
Clarity/Organization— *clearly expresses and logically develops ideas*	10	_____
Language mechanics— *uses proper spelling, grammar, and style*	10	_____
Correct format— *includes introduction, supporting paragraphs, and conclusion*	10	_____
TOTAL	**80**	_____

Comments: _____

_____

_____

Part A Score _____   Part B Score _____   **TOTAL SCORE** _____

16

DBQ THEME: THE CIVIL RIGHTS MOVEMENT

DIRECTIONS:

This task is based on the accompanying documents (1–9). Some of these documents have been edited to help you with the task. The essay is designed to test your ability to work with historical documents and your knowledge of the Civil Rights movement. Carefully analyze the documents as you complete **Part A**. Your responses should help you to write the essay in **Part B**.

HISTORICAL CONTEXT:

For generations, African Americans struggled for freedom and justice in the United States. This struggle for civil rights reached a high point in the 1950s and 1960s. This movement, led by several talented and popular leaders, such as Dr. Martin Luther King, Jr., forced the nation to take a look at race relations in America. Many changes were brought about as a result of the Civil Rights movement, but there are some who question whether these changes went far enough.

TASK:

- Describe the goals of the Civil Rights movement.
- Discuss at least two positive changes that occurred as a result of this movement.
- Discuss at least two ways in which the Civil Rights movement did not end America's race problems.

PART A—SHORT-ANSWER SECTION

The following documents relate to the Civil Rights movement. Examine each document carefully and answer the questions that follow.

Document 1: The March on Washington (1963)

Courtesy National Archives

More than 200,000 people participated in the March on Washington, D.C. on August 28, 1963. In this photograph, some of the organizers of the event lead the march. Dr. Martin Luther King, Jr. is seen in the front row, second from the left.

1. Name two things that these protesters demanded at the March on Washington.

_____

_____

_____(2)

May be copied for classroom use. *Teaching and Using Document-Based Questions for Middle School* by Edward O'Connor (Portsmouth, NH: Teacher Ideas Press); ©2004.

THE CIVIL RIGHTS MOVEMENT

Document 2: Dr. Martin Luther King, Jr. "I Have a Dream" (1963)

Five score years ago, a great American in whose shadow we stand signed the Emancipation Proclamation. This momentous decree came as a great beacon light of hope to millions of Negro slaves who had been seared in the flames of withering injustice. It came as a joyous daybreak to end the long night of captivity.

But one hundred years later, we must face the tragic fact that the Negro is still not free. One hundred years later, the life of the Negro is still sadly crippled by the chains of discrimination. One hundred years later, the Negro lives on a lonely island of poverty in the midst of a vast ocean of prosperity. One hundred years later, the Negro is still suffering in the corners of American society and finds himself an exile in his own land. So we have come here today to dramatize a terrible condition.

We have also come to this hallowed spot to remind America of the fierce urgency of now. Now is the time to rise from the dark and desolate valley of segregation to the sunlit path of racial justice. Now is the time to open the doors of opportunity to all of God's children. Now is the time to lift our nation from the quicksand of racial injustice to the solid rock of brotherhood.

Dr. King delivered this speech on the steps of the Lincoln Memorial at the March on Washington.

1. According to Dr. King, what are two reasons why "the Negro still is not free"?

_____

_____

_____

_____

_____(2)

2. According to this speech, what were two reasons for the March on Washington?

_____

_____

_____

_____

_____(2)

Document 3: Chart—Civil Rights Laws

CIVIL RIGHTS LAWS OF THE 1960'S	
CIVIL RIGHTS ACT OF 1964	Made it illegal to discriminate in hotels, restaurants, parks and other public places. Made discrimination illegal in hiring and education. Created the Equal Employment Opportunity Commission to help enforce this law.
THE 24TH AMENDMENT	Abolished poll taxes for federal elections. (Poll taxes were used to prevent African Americans from voting.)
VOTING RIGHTS ACT OF 1965	Ended restrictions on voting like literacy tests and poll taxes in all state elections. Allowed the federal government to register voters in states where there was discrimination.
CIVIL RIGHTS ACT OF 1968	Made it illegal to discriminate against people in the sale and rental of houses.

1. What government agency was created during the 1960s to help fight discrimination?

_____

_____

_____

_____

_____(1)

2. Which law banned discrimination in public places?

_____

_____

_____

_____(1)

Document 4: Before and After the Voting Rights Act

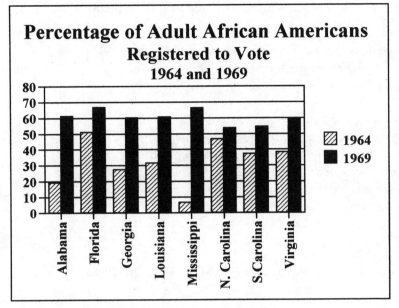

Source: Patterson, James T., America in the Twentieth Century

1. What does this graph show about the change in voter registration among African Americans in the south between 1964 and 1969?

_____

_____

_____

_____

_____(1)

2. What does this graph suggest about the Voting Rights Act of 1965?

_____

_____

_____

_____(1)

Document 5: Executive Order Number 11246 (1965)

The following is an executive order issued by President Lyndon B. Johnson on September 28, 1965.

It is the policy of the government of the United States to provide an equal opportunity in Federal employment for all qualified persons, to prohibit discrimination due to race, religion, color or national origin, and to encourage equal employment through a positive, continuing program in each department and agency.

Any company doing business with the Federal government will not discriminate against any employee or person applying for a job because of race, religion, color, or national origin. The company will take affirmative action to make sure that applicants are hired and treated during employment without regard to their race, religion, color or national origin. Such action shall include hiring, promotion, actively seeking individuals for hire, rates of pay, and training.

1. According to this executive order, what is the employment policy of the U.S. government?

_____

_____

_____

_____

_____(1)

2. Name at least two things that are required of companies that do business with the federal government, according to this order. _____

_____

_____

_____

_____(2)

Document 6: A Description of Busing

In the early 1970s, blacks and whites lived in separate sections of cities, and therefore attended separate neighborhood schools. This is known as de facto segregation, which basically means segregation by choice and/or circumstance, i.e. economic status. Many people thought this was a problem that could be solved by busing students to schools outside of their neighborhoods, thereby mixing students of different races. Below is the account of Phyllis Ellison, who experienced busing first hand.

> *I remember my first day going on the bus to South Boston High School. I wasn't afraid because I felt important. I didn't know what to expect, what was waiting for me up the hill. We had police escorts. I think there were three motorcycle cops and two police cruisers in front of the bus, and so I really felt important at that time, not knowing what was on the other side of the hill.*
>
> *Well, when we started up the hill, you could hear people saying "Go home!" There were signs they had made saying, "Black people stay out. We don't want any of you in our school." And there were people on the corners holding bananas like we were apes or monkeys. "Monkeys get out; get them out of our neighborhood. We don't want you in our schools." So at that time it did frighten me somewhat, but I was more determined then to get inside South Boston High School, because of the people that were outside.*

1. Explain why there was such angry protest over busing at South Boston High School, according to

this passage. _____

_____

_____

_____

_____(1)

Document 7: Thoughts on Racism in America

I am not suggesting that most whites are racist. The majority of them are certainly not. If a racist is defined as anyone who hates blacks (or members of any racial group, for that matter), the number of true racists is very small, and most of them are the pathetic sorts who call themselves Nazis and glorify the Ku Klux Klan. The point here is that people do not have to be racist in order to make decisions that unfairly harm members of another race. America is filled with attitudes, assumptions, stereotypes, and behaviors that make it practically impossible for blacks to believe that the nation is serious about its promise of equality.

When she announced that she was leaving her job at a Fortune 500 company, my friend, a young black woman and Harvard graduate, was pulled aside by one of her bosses. Why, the executive wanted to know, was the company having such a difficult time keeping young black professionals? The woman's frustrations were numerous. Rather than try to explain, the woman blurted out that there was "no one who looks like me" in all of senior management—by which she meant there were no blacks, and certainly no black women. "What reason do I have to believe," she added, "that I can make it to the top?"

When she related this story to me several years later, she remained discouraged. "The bottom line is you're black. And that's still a negative in this society."

1. According to the author, what is the effect of American attitudes and stereotypes regarding race?

_____

_____

_____

_____

_____(1)

2. Why did the author's friend feel that she could never rise to the top at her job?

_____

_____

_____

_____

_____(1)

Document 8: A Comparison of Income

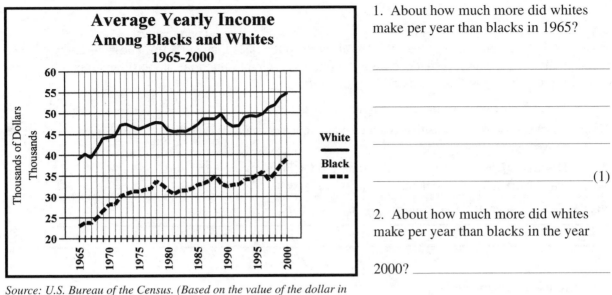

Average Yearly Income Among Blacks and Whites 1965-2000

Source: U.S. Bureau of the Census. (Based on the value of the dollar in the year 2000.)

1. About how much more did whites make per year than blacks in 1965?

_____

_____

_____

_____(1)

2. About how much more did whites make per year than blacks in the year

2000? _____

_____

_____(1)

Document 9: Thoughts on the Civil Rights Movement

"Nothing has changed!" In the past, I heard this statement from young African American students. I attributed such ignorance to their having been born too late to know what life, especially in the South, was like during the pre-1960s. But now I hear this from some who were themselves involved in the Civil Rights Movement of the '60s. And I ask, does it mean nothing that today African Americans have access to education, public places, and the ballot, the same as do European Americans? These are powerful tools which every American today can use to bring about continued advancement.

Anyone who says "Nothing has changed" must have forgotten or never have known the daily humiliations, not to mention the powerless position of blacks in our Southern culture before the 1960s.

1. Name at least two achievements of the Civil Rights movement mentioned in the selection above.

_____

_____

_____

_____(2)

NAME _____ DATE _____

PART B—ESSAY: THE CIVIL RIGHTS MOVEMENT

TASK:

Using the documents in your packet, your answers to the questions in Part A, and your knowledge of social studies, write a well-developed essay that includes an introduction, supporting paragraphs, and a conclusion in which you thoroughly address the following:

- Describe the goals of the Civil Rights movement.
- Discuss at least two positive changes that occurred as a result of this movement.
- Discuss at least two ways in which the Civil Rights movement did not end America's race problems.

NOTE: *your essay will be evaluated using the form below.*

	Point Value	Points Earned
Effective use of documents— *uses at least **5** documents*	15	_____
Accuracy— *includes correct information*	15	_____
Depth and detail— *supports main ideas with facts*	10	_____
Knowledge of social studies— *uses information beyond supplied documents*	10	_____
Clarity/Organization— *clearly expresses and logically develops ideas*	10	_____
Language mechanics— *uses proper spelling, grammar, and style*	10	_____
Correct format— *includes introduction, supporting paragraphs, and conclusion*	10	_____
TOTAL	**80**	_____

Comments: _____

_____

_____

Part A Score _____   Part B Score _____   **TOTAL SCORE** _____

APPENDIX I

RUBRIC FOR SCAFFOLDING QUESTIONS

This rubric is intended to serve as a quick reference for teachers, and will, I hope, save them time during the rating process. Many of the questions found in the scaffolding require students to list or name items found in the documents or to identify some statistical data. These answers are usually straightforward, and an answer key such as this can be useful and effective. In some cases, there are a number of ways that students can correctly respond, and so only some of the possible responses are listed.

Some questions, however, require students to react to a document or interpret it in ways that can be difficult to anticipate. A rubric that limits possible student responses to such questions is inherently flawed and ineffective. As a result, some of the items found in this answer key list only a few possible responses and allow for other acceptable answers that must be evaluated individually by the teacher rating the scaffolding.

NATIVE AMERICAN CULTURES

Document 1: Native American Culture Chart

1. Inuit, Sioux
   (2 points for two correct answers, 1 point for one.)

2. Any two of the following, or other acceptable response:
   They hunted animals that were available in the Arctic: seals, whales, walruses . . . ; They made igloos of snow; They moved around constantly (frequently) in search of food.
   (2 points for two correct answers, 1 point for one.)

Document 2: Hohokum Irrigation Canals

1. They would use them for drinking water and irrigation of their crops.
   (2 points for two correct answers, 1 point for one.)

2. They lived in a dry area and needed water to survive.
   (1 point for any correct response.)

Document 3: Making Canoes in Virginia

1. Possible responses include: They are easily carried over land if they are light; so they can use them again if more water gets in their way.
   (1 point for any correct response.)

2. Correct responses include two of the following: bark, trees, birch trees, sticks, clay, mud
   (2 points for two correct answers, 1 point for one.)

Document 4: Description of a Native American Home

1. Used to tie the willow saplings and straw together to make the home.
   Boards for the beds/bunks were tied together with buffalo hide.
   (2 points for two correct answers, 1 point for one.)

2. Possible responses include: They built their home with materials that were available to them ("close at hand"); they made good homes from materials that wouldn't have been useful to others.
   (1 point for any acceptable response.)

Document 5: Photograph of Cheyenne Tipis and Travois

1. They used travois to help them move their tipis and belongings.
   (1 point for any acceptable response.)

2. They needed to move in order to follow the buffalo herds.
   (1 point for any acceptable response.)

Document 6: An Indian Boy's Training

1. Any two of the following: to be observant of nature; how to hunt the grizzly; how to approach the grizzly; how to outwit animals; or other acceptable response.
   (2 points for two correct answers, 1 point for one.)

2. Patience and skill
   (2 points for two correct answers, 1 point for one.)

THE AGE OF EXPLORATION

Document 1: Description of Beijing, China by Marco Polo

1. Possible responses include: Valuable items (precious stones, silk, and pearls) are sold there; there are fine ladies and nobles and soldiers attending to the Emperor; people come from all over to do business there.
   (1 point for any acceptable response.)

2. Any two of the following: precious stones, jewels, pearls, silk, cloth of gold
   (2 points for two correct answers, 1 point for one.)

Document 2: A Caravel

1. Possible responses include: the sail, the lateen, the rudder
   (1 point for any acceptable response.)

Document 3: Hernan Cortes Calls for Volunteers

1. A share of the gold and grants of land.
   (2 points for two correct answers, 1 point for one.)

2. Any two of the following: weapons, horses, armor
   (2 points for two correct answers, 1 point for one.)

Document 4: The Astrolabe

1. The astrolabe helped explorers find their latitude at sea.
   (1 point for any acceptable response.)

Document 5: Excerpt from *A Brief Account of the Devastation of the Indies*

1. Possible responses include: People were killed; people died in captivity; people were sold off as slaves.
   (2 points for two correct answers, 1 point for one.)

2. Possible responses: 12 million; 15 million; between 12 and 15 million.
   (1 point for any acceptable response.)

Document 6: A Slave Factory in Africa

1. Because after being brought to the fortress, slaves were boarded onto slave ships.
   (1 point for any acceptable response.)

Document 7: An Argument for Colonization

1. Lumber could be used for masts, to build ships, or make navies.
   (1 point for any acceptable response.)

2. Possible responses include: Prevent the Spanish from taking over all of North America; stop them from using ports in lands that England claimed; build navies; make it difficult for them to bring their treasure into Europe . . .
   (2 points for two correct answers, 1 point for one.)

Document 8: The Colombian Exchange

1. Any two of the following: beans, cacao, corn, peppers, potatoes, squash, sunflowers, tomatoes.
   (2 points for two correct answers, 1 point for one.)

2. Any two of the following: plague, chicken pox, cold, influenza, measles, scarlet fever, smallpox
   (2 points for two correct answers, 1 point for one.)

DEMOCRACY IN COLONIAL AMERICA

Document 1: Maryland's Act of Toleration

1. Possible responses include: enforcing matters of religion is dangerous; for a more peaceful and quiet government; to maintain love and friendship in the colony.
   (1 point for any acceptable response.)

2. Freedom of religion
   (1 point for any acceptable response.)

3. Possible responses include: non-Christians, Jews, Muslims, Native Americans
   (1 point for any acceptable response.)

Document 2: Voting Qualifications

1. Any two of the following: being Christian, white, male, and either owning or renting property.
   (2 points for two correct answers, 1 point for one.)

2. Any two of the following: non-Christians, Jews, African Americans, Native Americans, women, poor people, people without property.
   (2 points for two correct answers, 1 point for one.)

Document 3: The Fundamental Orders of Connecticut

1. Any two of the following: to make laws, levy taxes, dispose of unclaimed land, call public officials into question, and remove and punish offenders.
    (2 points for two correct answers, 1 point for one.)

2. Any two of the following: The governor is elected; the governor is term-limited; the General Court (legislature) makes laws and taxes; public officials can be removed.
    (2 points for two correct answers, 1 point for one.)

3. Any two of the following: The governor has a term limit; if the governor doesn't call the General Court, the people can do it; the governor can be removed from office.
    (2 points for two correct answers, 1 point for one.)

Document 4: Title Page from *The Lady's Law*

1. The husband gained possession of it.
    (1 point for any acceptable response.)

2. Acceptable responses include: Women were legally dependent on their husbands; property went to husbands after marriage; inheritance was limited; they could not own property; they could not earn wages.
    (1 point for any acceptable response.)

Document 5: Plan of a Slave Ship

1. Any two of the following: They were crammed onto the ship; they were forced to lie down right next to each other; they were put on shelves.
    (2 points for two correct answers, 1 point for one.)

2. Possible responses include: Slavery is undemocratic; slaves have no rights; slaves were prevented from reading and writing . . .
    (1 point for any acceptable response.)

Document 6: Engraving of Virginia's House of Burgesses

1. Possible responses include: people are speaking, listening, thinking, making laws . . .
    (1 point for any acceptable response.)

2. People elected representatives, representatives made laws . . .
    (1 point for any acceptable response.)

LOYALISTS AND PATRIOTS IN THE REVOLUTION

Document 1: The Boston Massacre

1. Any two of the following: The British are shooting at the Americans; the Americans look innocent— or seem unarmed; it is a violent scene; the British stand in front of the "Butcher's Hall" sign.
    (2 points for two correct answers, 1 point for one.)

Document 2: A Loyalist is Tarred and Feathered

1. Possible responses include: He was a Loyalist; he would not curse the king.
    (1 point for any acceptable response.)

2. Possible responses include: She criticizes the mob; she states that the colonies are lawless and that the government is hopeless.
    (1 point for any acceptable response.)

Document 3: The Continental Congress Explains the Need to Fight

1. Any two of the following: They felt disasters of fire, sword and famine; they were subjected to an unfair government; they refused to surrender their freedom; they did not want to live as slaves.
   (2 points for two correct answers, 1 point for one.)

2. Possible responses include: They would be forced to live as slaves; their freedom and liberty would be lost; they would be dishonored.
   (1 point for any acceptable response.)

Document 4: A Comparison of Strength

1. Possible responses include: They could spend 4.5 million pounds for Hessians; they could afford to have a large army and navy.
   (1 point for any acceptable response.)

2. Students should receive one point for identifying Britain or the United States, and one point for an acceptable explanation. Example: Great Britain, because their army was better trained and equipped.

Document 5: A Description of the Continental Army

1. Any two of the following: they don't have proper clothes; soldiers are unhappy with Congress; there are disagreements and jealousies between New Englanders and Southerners.
   (2 points for two correct answers, 1 point for one.)

2. Possible responses include: they are not united; they are fighting among themselves; without proper clothes soldiers could get sick . . .
   (1 point for any acceptable response.)

Document 6: An Excerpt from *Common Sense*

1. Possible responses include: No one can set up his family to rule forever; it could put the next generation under the rule of a villain or a fool; people can't give away the rights of future generations.
   (1 point for any acceptable response.)

Document 7: An Excerpt from *Plain Truth*

1. Possible responses include: Britain is stronger; the colonies' army is weak; the colonies have no navy; Britain will not willingly let the colonies go . . .
   (2 points for two correct answers, 1 point for one.)

Document 8: Value of Trade with England

1. In 1771
   (1 point for any acceptable response.)

2. Possible responses include: Both imports and exports went down a great deal; there was less trade because of the war.
   (1 point for any acceptable response.)

Document 9: Song of the Minute Man

1. Possible responses include: for their country, for liberty, because their cause is just, for glory . . .
   (2 points for two correct answers, 1 point for one.)

POLITICAL PARTIES AND THE NEW NATION

Document 1: Differences Between Hamilton and Jefferson

1. Possible responses include: Hamilton believed in a strong federal government and Jefferson believed in strong state government; Hamilton believed in loose interpretation of the Constitution and Jefferson interpreted it strictly.
   (2 points for two correct answers, 1 point for one.)

2. He supported a strong federal government.
   (1 point for any acceptable response.)

Document 2: Hamilton Criticizes his Opponents

1. Possible responses include: They are a threat to good government; they are dangerous to the union as well as the peace and happiness of the country; they are attached to France and opposed to Great Britain.
   (2 points for two correct answers, 1 point for one.)

2. Possible responses include: he has a womanish attachment to France, he is dangerous, his loyalty is questionable, he might take advantage of disorder and seize power . . .
   (2 points for two correct answers, 1 point for one.)

Document 3: Jefferson on Parties

1. Individual differences in the way people think and unlimited freedom of expression.
   (2 points for two correct answers, 1 point for one.)

Document 4: Election Advertisement

1. Any two of the following: They support (are loyal to) Great Britain; they work for King George III; they want to enslave people and raise taxes.
   (2 points for two correct answers, 1 point for one.)

Document 5: The Sedition Act

1. Possible responses include: Writing, speaking, or publishing false, injurious, or harmful things about members of Congress or the president.
   (2 points for two correct answers, 1 point for one.)

2. One could not speak out against his opponent; one could not criticize his opponent.
   (1 point for any acceptable response.)

Document 6: The Death of Alexander Hamilton

1. Political rivalry led to violence; differences led to the duel . . .
   (1 point for any acceptable response.)

Document 7: A Letter to Massachusetts Voters

1. Governor and Senators
   (2 points for two correct answers, 1 point for one.)

2. Possible responses include: Because he is for peace; because he is against war with Britain.
   (1 point for any acceptable response.)

Document 8: Political Cartoon—The Gerrymander

1. Possible responses include: Elbridge Gerry's Congressional district; the practice of gerrymandering.
   (1 point for any acceptable response.)

2. Possible responses include: It gives one party an advantage in an election; it is undemocratic . . .
   (1 point for any acceptable response.)

DIFFERENCES BETWEEN THE NORTH AND THE SOUTH

Document 1: Colonial Slave Imports

1. South Carolina
   (1 point for a correct response)

2. Massachusetts
   (1 point for a correct response)

3. Possible responses include: Southern colonies imported far more slaves than the North.
   (1 point for any acceptable response.)

Document 2: A Letter from Thomas Jefferson to John Adams

1. Any two of the following: sheep/wool, cotton, hemp, flax
   (2 points for two correct answers, 1 point for one.)

2. Possible responses include: Goods are being manufactured in Massachusetts, while in Virginia, they make goods at home/use little machinery.
   (1 point for any acceptable response.)

Document 3: Observations of a French Visitor to America

1. Possible responses include: Work is not honored in the South; trade and industry thrive where there is no slavery.
   (1 point for any acceptable response.)

2. Trade and industry flourish more; wealth will pile up more in the North.
   (1 point for any acceptable response.)

Document 4: A Cotton Plantation

1. Possible responses include: farming, picking cotton
   (1 point for any acceptable response.)

2. Possible responses include: slaves, African Americans
   (1 point for any acceptable response.)

Document 5: A Description of Lowell, Massachusetts

1. Possible responses include: water, waterfalls, canals, the Western Suffolk Canal
   (2 points for two correct answers, 1 point for one.)

2. Possible responses include: Many new businesses started in Lowell between 1828 and 1832; 1,459,000 yards of cloth were produced there.
   (2 points for two correct answers, 1 point for one.)

Document 6: A View of Pittsburgh, Pennsylvania

1. Any two of the following: steam ship, boat, horse, wagon, cart, railroad, walking
   (2 points for two correct answers, 1 point for one.)

2. Any two of the following: loading, transporting, cutting, sawing wood
   (2 points for two correct answers, 1 point for one.)

Document 7: A Speech by Senator Robert Young Hayne of South Carolina

1. Possible responses include: to strengthen the union; for a more perfect union.
    (2 points for two correct answers, 1 point for one.)

2. Possible responses include: He fears that the federal government is becoming too powerful; he fears the states are losing power; he fears a government with unlimited power.
    (1 point for any acceptable response.)

Document 8: Massachusetts Senator Daniel Webster's Response to Hayne

1. The people can change/amend the Constitution whenever they choose.
    (1 point for any acceptable response.)

2. Any two of the following: happiness and prosperity have grown because of the Constitution; it cannot be overthrown, undermined, or nullified; because of the Constitution, we enjoy safety at home and dignity abroad.
    (2 points for two correct answers, 1 point for one.)

Document 9: South Carolina's Ordinance of Nullification

1. Any two of the following: the Constitution doesn't allow Congress to protect Northern manufactures; Congress must impose taxes equally; they are unconstitutional.
    (2 points for two correct answers, 1 point for one.)

2. They do not have to obey the Tariffs of 1828 and 1832.
    (1 point for any acceptable response.)

SLAVERY IN THE UNITED STATES

Document 1: A Speech by Frederick Douglass

1. Any two of the following: they are owned, master has absolute power, master may work him, hire him out, kill him.
    (2 points for two correct answers, 1 point for one.)

2. Any two of the following: to ensure good behavior, motivation to work, to destroy manhood.
    (2 points for two correct answers, 1 point for one.)

Document 2: Auction Advertisement

1. Any two: land, corn, other property
    (2 points for two correct answers, 1 point for one.)

2. Possible responses: they are property; they are things to be owned and sold.
    (1 point for any acceptable response.)

Document 3: Georgia Asks for Slavery

1. Possible responses include: It would give them cheap labor; they could make more money.
    (1 point for any acceptable response.)

2. Possible responses: plant the land, manufacture timber, load ships.
    (1 point for any acceptable response.)

Document 4: Voyage to America on a Slave Ship

1. Because they did not want to be slaves; or, they preferred death to slavery.
    (1 point for any acceptable response.)

Document 5: Devices of Slavery

1. To keep them from running away; to punish them; to keep them from eating crops; or other acceptable response.
   (2 points for two correct answers, 1 point for one.)

2. Possible responses: They caused pain; they were uncomfortable; they made it hard to breathe.
   (1 point for any acceptable response.)

Document 6: A Speech Defending Slavery

1. Production of cotton depends on slavery.
   (1 point for any acceptable response.)

2. He states that Africans are inferior, that they aren't fit to be free; it is marked on the skin.
   (1 point for any acceptable response.)

Document 7: Keeping Slave Families Together

1. Death, master's choice
   (2 points for two correct answers, 1 point for one.)

2. Possible responses include: the master played a major role; only death was greater; master far more important than personal choice.
   (1 point for any acceptable response.)

Document 8: Photograph of a Slave Who Was Whipped

1. Possible responses: They were treated harshly; beatings like this one were severe.
   (1 point for any acceptable response.)

Document 9: Description of a Slave Auction

1. Her son was sold; the man couldn't afford to buy them all; it was up to the master and not her . . .
   (1 point for any acceptable response.)

RECONSTRUCTION

Document 1: A Southerner Describes Politics During Reconstruction

1. Any two of the following: scalawags, carpetbaggers, Negroes
   (2 points for two correct answers, 1 point for one.)

2. Any two of the following: prohibited imprisonment for debt; divided representatives according to population; created public schools; required attendance at school.
   (2 points for two correct answers, 1 point for one.)

Document 2: Illustration: "Everything Points to a Democratic Victory this Fall"

1. Possible responses include: threat of violence, the gun, separated from white voters, not allowed inside, the signs on the door.
   (2 points for two correct answers, 1 point for one.)

Document 3: A Freedman Describes His Experience

1. Any two of the following: He was tricked; they didn't know how to support themselves; they did not know how to save, or spend wisely; they had no money, no land.
   (2 points for two correct answers, 1 point for one.)

2. Possible responses include: The government didn't take care of Freedmen; the government didn't support them or feed them.
(1 point for any acceptable response.)

Document 4: Sharecropping

1. Labor was similar; sharecroppers worked for whites/former masters; sharecroppers were unable to make money.
(2 points for two correct answers, 1 point for one.)

Document 5: Illustration: "Worse Than Slavery"

1. Ku Klux Klan, White League, white people
(2 points for two correct answers, 1 point for one.)

2. Any two of the following: violence, hanging, fire/burning, attacks by the KKK/White League, terrorized.
(2 points for two correct answers, 1 point for one.)

Document 6: A Tennessee Family Moves West

1. To improve his financial situation; to be with other people from Tennessee.
(1 point for any acceptable response.)

Document 7: Schools for Freedmen

1. Learning, reading, going to school.
(2 points for two correct answers, 1 point for one.)

Document 8: "A Yankee Visits the New South"

1. They have become industrial; they've gotten involved in business.
(1 point for any acceptable response.)

2. Any two of the following: iron, coal, lumber, marble
(2 points for two correct answers, 1 point for one.)

IMMIGRATION

Document 1: An Argument for Immigration

1. Any two of the following: Immigrants added wealth to society, built houses, dug canals, graded railroads, consumed food, made clothes.
(2 points for two correct answers, 1 point for one.)

2. Any/all of the following: strong mind, brave heart, self-respect, intelligence
(1 point for any acceptable response.)

Document 2: A Senator Speaks Out Against Immigration

1. Any two of the following: They combine to elect their own kind to Congress; they will create a foreign colony; they know nothing about our political system.
(2 points for two correct answers, 1 point for one.)

Document 3: Chinese Laborers, Humboldt Plains, Nevada

1. Working on the railroad.
(1 point for any acceptable response.)

Document 4: Memoir of David P. Conyngham, Civil War Soldier

1. Any two of the following: safety of the republic; principles of democracy; Constitution was in danger; because the U.S. gave the Irish shelter, they felt loyalty to the U.S.
   (2 points for two correct answers, 1 point for one.)

2. America took them in and protected/sheltered them.
   (1 point for any acceptable response.)

Document 5: Comments about Immigration in *Atlantic Monthly*

1. People dislike those who are different; they blame immigrants for strikes, fights, the turn of an election.
   (2 points for two correct answers, 1 point for one.)

2. People have gotten used to them.
   (1 point for any acceptable response.)

Document 6: Political Cartoon

1. Themselves or their fathers when they were immigrants.
   (1 point for any acceptable response.)

2. Possible responses include: He is poor; he is dressed poorly.
   (1 point for any acceptable response.)

Document 7: The Immigrant Invasion

1. Because they work at low wages, or, their labor is cheap.
   (1 point for any acceptable response.)

2. Immigrants took jobs of natural born workers; they harmed standard of living; they spread poverty; they crowded slums.
   (1 point for any acceptable response.)

Document 8: Chart

1. Felix Frankfurter
   (1 point)

Document 9: "A Jewish Search for Freedom"

1. Possible responses include: They all came over the same way, in the same condition, with bundles and bags, all seeking a better life.
   (1 point for any acceptable response.)

2. Any two of the following: garment industry, jewelry, retail, medical and dental professions.
   (2 points for two correct answers, 1 point for one.)

THE GROWTH OF INDUSTRY

Document 1: Andrew Carnegie—*Wealth*

1. Any two of the following: goods are of higher quality, prices are better, poor enjoy luxuries, standard of living is better.
   (2 points for two correct answers, 1 point for one.)

2. Worker and employer don't work together or know each other; wages are low; there is friction between worker and employer.
   (2 points for two correct answers, 1 point for one.)

Document 2: Wealth's Influence on Government

1. Any two of the following: wealth corrupts governments, supports the ruling party, buys off government.
   (2 points for two correct answers, 1 point for one.)

Document 3: The Rise of Labor Unions

1. Answers should range between 2,000,000 and 2,300,000.
   (1 point for any acceptable response.)

Document 4: A Visit to the Steel Mills at Homestead, Pa.

1. Any two of the following: iron explodes, slag falls on them, carriers and cranes moving.
   (2 points for two correct answers, 1 point for one.)

2. Possible responses: 12 hours of work, no time for anything else, 14 cents per hour
   (2 points for two correct answers, 1 point for one.)

Document 5: Photograph of a Georgia Cotton Mill

1. Possible responses include: climbing on the spinning frame, mending broken threads, putting back empty bobbins.
   (1 point for any acceptable response.)

2. Child labor, children in danger, working a dangerous job
   (1 point for any acceptable response.)

Document 6: Women at Work

1. Women were able to take care of themselves, were less dependent on men.
   (1 point for any acceptable response.)

Document 7: The Memoirs of John D. Rockefeller

1. Standard Oil
   (1 point)

2. Any two of the following: His company supplies oil to people throughout the country; prices have decreased; the company brings money into the country.
   (2 points for two correct answers, 1 point for one.)

Document 8: Description of a Coal Mine

1. Any two of the following: being crushed, gas, floods, cars "shooting" through the tunnel, "miner's asthma".
   (2 points for two correct answers, 1 point for one.)

Document 9: Steel Production at the End of the Nineteenth Century

1. It rose for the most part, increasing by 11 million tons.
   (1 point for any acceptable response.)

THE PROGRESSIVE ERA

Document 1: Passages from *The History of the Standard Oil Company*

1. Any two of the following: railroad rebates, restraint of trade, monopoly
   (2 points for two correct answers, 1 point for one.)

2. Any two of the following: He caused oil stills to be deserted, made national life poorer, uglier, meaner . . .
(2 points for two correct answers, 1 point for one.)

Document 2: *The Jungle* by Upton Sinclair

1. Any two of the following: meat was on the floor; meat stored in leaky rooms with rats climbing on it; rat dung in meat; poisoned bread combined with the meat.
(2 points for two correct answers, 1 point for one.)

Document 3: Theodore Roosevelt Proposes a Law

1. The sale of contaminated or polluted food, or the mislabeling of food, drinks, and drugs.
(1 point for any acceptable response.)

2. It would protect the health and welfare of the public.
(1 point for any acceptable response.)

Document 4: Laws of the Progressive Era

1. Any two of the following: outlawed railroad rebates, set railroad rates, required businesses to list ingredients, outlawed false advertising.
(2 points for two correct answers, 1 point for one.)

2. Publicity Act
(1 point)

Document 5: Headlines from the *New York Times*

1. Standard Oil and Tobacco Trust
(2 points for two correct answers, 1 point for one.)

2. They were dissolved, broken up.
(1 point for any acceptable response.)

Document 6: Meat Inspection Act

1. Any two of the following: Meat is an important source of food, consumed throughout the nation; unhealthy meat can injure the public . . .
(2 points for two correct answers, 1 point for one.)

2. It will prevent poisonous/harmful substances from being included in meat products.
(1 point for any acceptable response.)

Document 7: Two Progressive Amendments

1. The power to collect income tax.
(1 point)

2. The power to elect senators.
(1 point)

Document 8: Women's Suffrage in New York State

1. They won the right to vote.
(1 point for any acceptable response.)

AMERICA IN THE 1920S

Document 1: *Life* Magazine Cover

1. Possible responses include: the people are well dressed; he is wearing a tuxedo; she is wearing jewelry.
   (2 points for two correct answers, 1 point for one.)

Document 2: A Poem by Langston Hughes

1. They were excluded, left out, denied opportunities.
   (1 point for any acceptable response.)

2. That soon they would be included and appreciated, they would grow stronger.
   (1 point for any acceptable response.)

Document 3: Statement by Bartolomeo Vanzetti

1. Possible responses include: There was widespread prejudice against foreigners and radicals at that time; the court stirred up those prejudices; the jury was biased.
   (2 points for two correct answers, 1 point for one.)

2. He was radical and Italian.
   (2 points for two correct answers, 1 point for one.)

Document 4: A Criticism of Prohibition

1. At least $75 million per year in New York State alone.
   (1 point for any acceptable response.)

2. Possible responses include: armies of bootleggers and moonshiners, corrupt government officials, a state of lawlessness.
   (1 point for any acceptable response.)

Document 5: Swimsuits of the 20s

1. Possible responses include: some are sleeveless, others have short sleeves; some cover the legs and others do not.
   (1 point for any acceptable response.)

2. Possible responses: These are more like dresses; these cover more/reveal less.
   (1 point for any acceptable response.)

Document 6: A Declaration of the Ku Klux Klan

1. 1866, during Reconstruction.
   (1 point for any acceptable response.)

2. Any two of the following: protecting women, maintaining white supremacy, honoring the achievements of their fathers, protecting their rights and privileges.
   (2 points for two correct answers, 1 point for one.)

Document 7: The Candidacy of Al Smith

1. It was the first time in U.S. history that religion was an issue.
   (1 point for any acceptable response.)

Document 8: Anti-Lynching Advertisement

1. Possible responses: People are burned at the stake; 3436 people were lynched between 1889 and 1922.
   (1 point for any acceptable response.)

2. Support the Anti-Lynching Bill, contact their Senator.
   (1 point for any acceptable response.)

Document 9: Line Graphs—Automobiles and Radios

1. Radios
   (1 point)

2. About 3 million more.
   (1 point for any acceptable response.)

THE GREAT DEPRESSION AND THE NEW DEAL

Document 1: A Chart of Some New Deal Programs

1. Any two: CCC, PWA, WPA
   (2 points for two correct answers, 1 point for one.)

2. Any two of the following: farmers, young men, the unemployed, bank depositors, investors, artists, actors, writers, builders.
   (2 points for two correct answers, 1 point for one.)

Document 2: Oral History: Gardiner C. Means

1. Any two of the following: it changed attitudes of businesses and the public; it gave people hope that something could be done; industrial production went up.
   (2 points for two correct answers, 1 point for one.)

2. Government took a role in industry, in the economy . . .
   (1 point for any acceptable response.)

Document 3: A Letter to FDR in Response to a "Fireside Chat"

1. Any two of the following: She is better off; her brother got a job; she has greater job security; the president is interested; he has not forgotten the people; his programs are sincere.
   (2 points for two correct answers, 1 point for one.)

Document 4: The Civilian Conservation Corps at Work

1. Possible responses include: planting, cleaning up the highway, digging, gardening.
   (1 point for any acceptable response.)

2. They got jobs, were employed, and were able to make money . . .
   (1 point for any acceptable response.)

Document 5: A 1960 Interview with George Bigge

1. Any two of the following: Federal government tried to solve social and economic problems; government spent a lot of money on Social Security programs; people asked/expected the government to solve their problems; government's relationship to individual needs changed.
   (2 points for two correct answers, 1 point for one.)

Document 6: Oral History—David Kennedy

1. World War II, the war
   (1 point for any acceptable response.)

2. Any two of the following: took care of immediate suffering; it gave people hope; it saved the country from collapse.
   (2 points for two correct answers, 1 point for one.)

Document 7: Line Graph—Unemployment

1. 1933
   (1 point)

2. Between 1942–1943
   (1 point)

Document 8: Oral History—Ben Isaacs

1. Possible responses include: He struggled living day to day, couldn't pay the rent, had to sell car, had to go on relief . . .
   (1 point for any acceptable response.)

2. He didn't want to take money from anyone; he was ashamed to be on relief.
   (1 point for any acceptable response.)

AMERICA IN WORLD WAR II

Document 1: President Roosevelt's Annual Message to Congress

1. Possible responses include: Being superior in weapons; out-producing the enemy.
   (1 point for any acceptable response.)

2. Any two of the following: converting factories/tools to war production; diverting raw materials to war production; limiting and/or cutting civilian use of some resources.
   (2 points for two correct answers, 1 point for one.)

Document 2: Photo of a War Production Plant

1. Airplanes
   (1 point for any acceptable response.)

2. The U.S. can produce many planes at once.
   (1 point for any acceptable response.)

Document 3: Scrap Drive Poster

1. Scrap metal, scrap, or metal
   (1 point for any acceptable response.)

2. Building tanks, ships, guns
   (1 point for any acceptable response.)

Document 4: Lend-Lease Agreement

1. Defense of the United Kingdom is vital to the defense of the U.S.
   (1 point for any acceptable response.)

2. Any two of the following: defense articles, services, information
   (2 points for two correct answers, 1 point for one.)

Document 5: Line Graph—War Production

1. 30 thousand
   (1 point)

2. Possible responses: It rose a great deal; It went up sharply.
   (*1 point for any acceptable response.*)

Document 6: War Bond Poster

1. Possible responses include: making bombs, artillery, equipment
   (*1 point for any acceptable response.*)

Document 7: Bar Graph—Airplanes Produced and Lost

1. Japan
   (*1 point*)

2. The U.S. produced more, and therefore could afford more losses.
   (*1 point for any acceptable response.*)

Document 8: Wartime Production Poster

1. Come up with and share ideas to make work go more quickly.
   (*1 point for any acceptable response.*)

2. It made them feel that they could help shorten the war.
   (*1 point for any acceptable response.*)

Document 9: World War II Statistics

1. Soviet Union
   (*1 point*)

2. America suffered fewer casualties than its allies, but spent more money.
   (*2 points for both casualties and spending, 1 point for only one.*)

AMERICA AND THE COLD WAR

Document 1: Assessment of the Soviet Union by George F. Kennan

1. Any two of the following: to disrupt the harmony of our society; to destroy our way of life; to break our international power.
   (*2 points for two correct answers, 1 point for one.*)

2. As thoroughly and carefully as if it were a war, as if we were at war.
   (*1 point for any acceptable response.*)

Document 2: Fallout Shelter

1. To protect people from a nuclear attack; to protect people from fallout.
   (*1 point for any acceptable response.*)

2. Possible responses include: They believed that a nuclear attack was likely; they knew that fallout was dangerous.
   (*1 point for any acceptable response.*)

Document 3: American Reaction to Sputnik

1. They worried that the U.S. had been passed by scientifically and militarily by the U.S.S.R.
   (*1 point for any acceptable response.*)

2. Possible responses include: plan to accomplish the next breakthrough; send up a manned satellite; get to the moon.
   (*1 point for any acceptable response.*)

Document 4: Military Training in the Cold War

1. They were training for fighting in a nuclear war.
   (1 point for any acceptable response.)

2. Danger from the explosion, radioactivity/fallout
   (1 point for any acceptable response.)

Document 5: A Statement to the House Un-American Activities Committee

1. They claimed he was sneaking communist ideas into films; they thought he was a communist.
   (1 point for any acceptable response.)

2. Possible responses include: They were conducting an illegal trial; they were smearing and humiliating people; they were trying to destroy him; they were trying to keep him from working.
   (1 point for any acceptable response.)

Document 6: Soviet News Service Report on the U-2 Spy Plane Incident

1. Statements by President Eisenhower and Vice President Nixon
   (1 point for any acceptable response.)

2. It could lead to the use of nuclear weapons/a nuclear war; it could lead to catastrophic consequences . . .
   (1 point for any acceptable response.)

Document 7: "Duck and Cover Drills"

1. They are preparing for a nuclear attack/air raid.
   (1 point for any acceptable response.)

Document 8: John F. Kennedy's Television Address Regarding the Cuban Missile Crisis

1. Nuclear weapons are destructive and swift; they would be able to strike major cities in the Western Hemisphere; they can carry warheads more than 1000 miles.
   (2 points for two correct answers, 1 point for one.)

2. Attack the Soviet Union.
   (1 point for any acceptable response.)

Document 9: The Arms Race

1. The U.S.
   (1 point)

2. The U.S.S.R.
   (1 point)

3. About 40–41 thousand
   (1 point for any acceptable response.)

THE CIVIL RIGHTS MOVEMENT

Document 1: The March on Washington

1. Any two of the following: jobs, equal rights, voting rights, end of segregation, decent pay
   (2 points for two correct answers, 1 point for one.)

Document 2: Dr. Martin Luther King, Jr. "I Have a Dream"

1. Any two of the following: discrimination, poverty, treated as an exile in his own land
    (2 points for two correct answers, 1 point for one.)

2. Any two of the following: to demand an end to segregation; to demand racial justice; to open doors of opportunity; to end racial injustice; to encourage brotherhood; to call attention to racial problems.
    (2 points for two correct answers, 1 point for one.)

Document 3: Chart—Civil Rights Laws

1. Equal Employment Opportunity Commission (EEOC)
    (1 point)

2. The Civil Rights Act of 1964
    (1 point)

Document 4: Before and After the Voting Rights Act

1. It increased in every southern state.
    (1 point for any acceptable response.)

2. It suggests that it was successful, that many people took advantage of the law.
    (1 point for any acceptable response.)

Document 5: Executive Order Number 11246

1. Possible responses: to provide equal opportunity regardless of race, color, religion; to prohibit discrimination; to encourage equal employment.
    (1 point for any acceptable response.)

2. Any two of the following: They will not discriminate; They will take affirmative action, make sure that people are hired, promoted, and treated regardless of their race.
    (2 points for two correct answers, 1 point for one.)

Document 6: A Description of Busing

1. Whites didn't want blacks in their school; people were racist.
    (1 point for any acceptable response.)

Document 7: Thoughts on Racism in America

1. They make it hard for African Americans to believe that America is serious about equality.
    (1 point for any acceptable response.)

2. There were no blacks/black women at high levels of the company.
    (1 point for any acceptable response.)

Document 8: A Comparison of Income

1. About 15 thousand dollars
    (1 point for any acceptable response.)

2. About 15 thousand dollars
    (1 point for any acceptable response.)

Document 9: Thoughts on the Civil Rights Movement

1. Any two of the following: access to education and other public places; voting rights; no longer subject to daily humiliations; no longer in powerless positions.
    (2 points for two correct answers, 1 point for one.)

APPENDIX II

INTERNET RESOURCES

Many teachers understand that using primary source documents in class can provide enriching experiences for their students, and that a great place to look for such documents is on the Internet. The following list is not intended to be a complete list of resources by any means. These sites, which I encountered while researching this book, can serve as a starting point for anyone interested in using primary source documents in the classroom.

GOVERNMENT SITES

1. American Memory—Library of Congress: http://memory.loc.gov
   This is a fantastic site! To call it a treasure trove is an understatement because it boasts over seven million digital items spread throughout more than one hundred collections. (Library of Congress home page: http://www.loc.gov)

2. Archival Research Catalog (ARC)—National Archives and Records Administration: http://www.archives.gov/research_room/arc/index.html
   An important site for anyone interested in primary source documents. The National Archives holds a tremendous number of textual and visual items created by the federal government. Searching through ARC (which replaced NAIL) will give you access to NARA's digital holdings, as well as those found in presidential libraries. (National Archives home page: http://www.archives.gov)

3. U.S. Census Bureau—Subjects Index: http://www.census.gov/acsd/www/subjects.html
   Current and recent historic statistical data can be found on this site. The subject index is very large, and many different statistics are available. A more comprehensive source for historical data can be found in print in *Historical Statistics of the United States: Colonial Times to 1970.* (Washington, DC: Government Printing Office, 1975)

4. U.S. Bureau of Labor Statistics: http://www.bls.gov
   A good source for statistics on the American work force.

5. Central Intelligence Agency—Electronic Reading Room: http://www.foica.cia.gov.
   Many declassified documents can be found here, having been made available by the Freedom of Information Act.

6. NASA—History Page: http://www.hq.nasa.gov/ofice/pao/History/history.html
   Contains documents relating to the space program.

7. Food and Drug Administration: http://www.fda.gov/opacom/laws/lawtoc.htm
   Contains the text of laws and other statutes enforced by the FDA.

8. Equal Employment Opportunity Commission: http://www.eeoc.gov/index.htm
   Contains the text of many Civil Rights laws and executive orders.

9. Social Security Administration—History Page: http://www.ssa.gov/history/history.html
   Even the Social Security Administration has a history site! This one has oral histories, a photo gallery, and more.

10. Federal Reserve Bank of Minneapolis—"What's a Dollar Worth?":
    http://woodrow.mpls.frb.fed.us/research/data/us/calc
    Features a calculator that will help you determine the value of a dollar from 1913 to 2002. There are also links to sites where you can figure out values before that.

The above resources represent just a few of the web sites maintained by the federal government. Just about every executive agency and department maintains its own, as well do the legislative and judicial branches of the U.S. government. There are also many states that have online documents through their respective state museums and archives.

ACADEMIC SITES

1. The American Presidency Project—University of California, Santa Barbara:
   http://www.presidency.ucsb.edu/index.html
   There are over 26,000 documents at this site relating to presidents of the United States. Features include State of the Union addresses from Washington to Clinton as well as inaugural addresses, up to and including George W. Bush.

2. American Studies at the University of Virginia: http://xroads.virginia.edu
   Many hypertexts are presented here: The journals of Lewis and Clark and *The Souls of Black Folk* by W. E. B. Du Bois are just two examples.

3. The Avalon Project at Yale Law School: http://www.yale.edu/lawweb/avalon/avalon.htm
   This extensive site includes primary source documents from ancient times (The Twelve Tables—450 B.C.) to the twenty-first century.

4. A Chronology of U.S. Historical Documents—University of Oklahoma College of Law:
   http://www.law.ou.edu/hist
   Precolonial documents (Magna Carta 1215) to the present.

5. Documenting the American South—University of North Carolina:
   http://docsouth.unc.edu/dasmain.html
   A great source for documents relating to southern history. There are more than 1160 items, including oral histories.

6. The Electronic Text Center—University of Virginia:
   http://etext.lib.virginia.edu/modeng0.browse.html
   Contains works of fiction, nonfiction, letters, illustrations, poetry, and much more. Documents range from the 1500s to the present.

7. George Mason University—Digitized Collections:
   http://www.gmu.edu/library/specialcollections/digitize.html
   Thousands of images are available through this site. There are photographs as well as Civil War era illustrations.

8. History Project—University of California, Davis:
   http://historyproject.ucdavis.edu/imageapplication/MarchandMajors.cfm
   A great source for visual documents. Professor Roland Marchand has assembled many slides on a wide variety of subjects.

9. A Hypertext on American History—University of Groningen, Netherlands:
   http://odur.let.rug.nl/~usa/d/index.htm
   This site is part of an interdepartmental project at the University of Groningen in the Netherlands. Art students and American Studies students created this site by gathering and posting essays and other primary source documents relating to American history.

10. Internet Medieval Sourcebook—Fordham University: http://www.fordham.edu/halsall/sbook.html
    This site is home to many primary source, public domain documents from the fall of Rome through the Age of Exploration.

11. Mount Holyoke College—International Relations Program:
    http://www.mtholyoke.edu/acad/intrel/feros-pg.htm
    A very extensive site with many primary source documents, especially relating to American foreign policy.

INDEPENDENT/COMMERCIAL SITES

1. Archiving Early America: http://www.earlyamerica.com/
   Provides a great deal of primary source material from the eighteenth century.

2. The Atlantic Online: http://www.theatlantic.com
   Of course you can read the current issue, but there is also an extensive archive section.

3. Bartleby.com: http://www.bartleby.com
   Although Bartleby is an Internet bookseller, it provides free access to many types of sources, primary and otherwise.

4. Britannia Historical Documents: http://www.britannia.com/history/docs/sourceshome
   This site promotes travel to Britain, but there are extensive documents on British history dating from A.D. 61 to the World War II era.

5. Gateway to Educational Materials: http://www.thegateway.org/welcome.html
   Sponsored by the U.S. Education Department, this organization's goal is to give educators quick and easy access to educational resources.

6. Harper's Weekly
   http://www.harpweek.com
   Harper's provides an excellent archive of their material online. There are interesting articles on and illustrations of slavery, the Civil War, and Reconstruction, as well as presidential elections and advertising from the nineteenth century.

7. History Central: http://www.multied.com
   This is a very informative site, with access to primary source documents and links.

8. The Loyal American Regiment: http://www.users.erols.com/candidus/reghist.htm
   This site carries a great deal of information and primary sources regarding loyalist soldiers during the Revolution. Documents include recruitment posters, songs, and other propaganda.

9. PBS: http://www.pbs.org

   Click on "Programs A–Z" and you will gain access to sites for many of the high-quality programs that have been featured on PBS. While these sites support the programs, they also carry special features, including primary source documents and other links and resources.

10. Union Pacific Railroad: http://www.uprr.com/aboutup/history

    The "History and Photos" section of this site is both interesting and useful for units involving westward expansion in the nineteenth century. A similar site for the Central Pacific Railroad can be found at: http://www.cprr.com/Museums/index.html

SOURCES FOR WORKS CITED

Chapter 1: Native American Cultures

Document 1: Kolata, Alan L., Donald L. Fixico and Sharlotte Neely. "Indian, American." *World Book Multimedia Encyclopedia.* CD-ROM World Book, 1997.

Kopper, Philip, *The Smithsonian Book of Native American Indians: Before the Coming of the Europeans* (Washington, D.C.: Smithsonian Books, 1986).

Document 2: Tiewes, Helga, "Snaketown Canals," from the collections of the Arizona State Museum, University of Arizona.

Document 3: Beverly, Robert. *The History and Present State of Virginia* (London: B. S. Toole, 1722). Reprinted by the Library of Congress, "The Capital and The Bay: Narratives of Washington and the Chesapeake Bay Region 1600–1925." *American Memory,* March 31, 2001. http://memory.loc.gov/ammem/lhcbhtml/lhcbhome/html.

Document 4: Coyler, Vincent, *Notes Among the Indians* (New Rochelle, N.Y.: G. P. Putnam's Sons, 1869). 475. Reprinted by the Electronic Text Center, University of Virginia Library, 1999. http://etext.lib.virginia.edu/modeng/modeng0.browse.html.

Document 5: "Pawnee Indians, Nebraska." Western History/Genealogy Department, Denver Public Library X-32649. Posted by the Library of Congress "History of the American West, 1860–1920: Photographs from the Collection of the Denver Public Library." *American Memory,* July 25, 2000. http://memory.loc.gov/ammem/award97/codhtml/hawphome.html.

Document 6: Eastman, Charles Alexander, *Indian Boyhood* (Omaha, Neb.: Univ. of Nebraska Press, 1902). 50–55. Reprinted by the Electronic Text Center, University of Virginia Library, 1999. http://etext.lib.virginia.edu/modeng/modeng0.browse.html.

(Permission to use passages from *Indian Boyhood* and *Notes Among the Indians* granted by the Rector and the Visitors of the University of Virginia and the Electronic Text Center.)

Chapter 2: The Age of Exploration

Document 1: Polo, Marco, *The Travels of Marco Polo,* trans. Teresa Waugh from the Italian by Maria Bellonci (New York: Facts on File, 1984), 86.

Document 2: Hiller, J. K., "The Portuguese Explorers." *Newfoundland and Labrador Heritage*, 1988, fig. http://heritagenf.ca/exploration/caravel.htm.

Document 3: Diaz del Castillo, Bernal, *The True History of the Conquest of Mexico* (Ann Arbor, Mich.: University Microfilms), 1966, 27.

Document 4: Morrison, James E., "The Mariner's Astrolabe." In *The Astrolabe: An Instrument with a Past and a Future,* June 5, 2002. http://astrolabes.org/MARINER.HTM

Document 5: Las Casas, Bartolome de. *A Brief Account of the Devastation of the Indies,* 1542. Reprinted by B. Dorsey, 1999. http://www.swarthmore.edu/socSci/bdorsey/41docs/02-las.html.

Document 6: "Slave Factories, or Compounds, Maintained by Traders . . ." Prints and Photographs Division, Library of Congress, LC-USZ62-106828.

Document 7: Hakluyt, Richard. *A Discourse Concerning Western Planting,* 1584. The Collections of the Maine Historical Society. Ser.2, vol. 2, 152–61. Reprinted by B. Dorsey, 1999. http://www.swarthmore.edu/SocSci/bdorsey1/41docs/03-hak.html.

Document 8: Carr, Ian, "Plagues and Peoples: The Columbian Exchange." *Hippocrates on the Web: History of Medicine, Faculty of Medicine, University of Manitoba*, March 6, 1998. http://www.umanitoba.ca/faculties/medicine/history/histories/plagues.html.

"The Columbian Exchange." http://english.ohio-state.edu/people/odlin.1/courses/571/columbex.htm.

Chapter 3: Democracy in Colonial America

Document 1: "An Act Concerning Religion, April 21, 1649." *The Archives of Maryland.* http://www.mdarchives.state.md.us/msa/speccol/sc2200/sc000025/html/transactrel.html.

Document 2: Purvis, Thomas L., *Colonial America to 1763* (New York: Facts on File, 1999), 193.

Document 3: "The Fundamental Orders of Connecticut," January 14, 1639. "University of Oklahoma College of Law: A Chronology of U.S. Historical Documents." *University of Oklahoma Law Center*, February 4, 2002. http://law.ou.edu/hist/orders.html.

Document 4: *The Lady's Law* 1733. Reprinted in Carter Smith, ed., *American Historical Images on File: Colonial and Revolutionary America* (New York: Facts on File, 1990), 3.25.

Document 5: "Stowage of the Slave Ship Brookes." Library of Congress, Prints and Photographs Division, LC-USZ62-44000.

Document 6: "The First Meeting of the House of Burgesses." Library of Congress, Prints and Photographs Division, LC-USZ62-890.

Chapter 4: Loyalists and Patriots in the Revolution

Document 1: Revere, Paul, "The Boston Massacre," 1775. Reprinted in: Thomas Fleming, *Liberty: The American Revolution.* (New York: Viking, 1997), 76.

Document 2: Hulton, Ann, *Letters of a Loyalist Lady* (New York: New York Times and Arno Press, 1971), 70–71.

Document 3: Jefferson, Thomas and John Dickenson, "A Declaration by the Representatives of the United Colonies of North America, Now Met in Congress at Philadelphia, Setting Forth the Causes and Necessity of their Taking up Arms." Arranged by Charles C. Tansill, *The Avalon Project at Yale Law School*, February 15, 2002. http://yale.edu/lawweb/avalon/arms.htm.

Document 4: Boatner, Mark Mayo III, *Encyclopedia of the American Revolution* (New York: David McKay Co. Inc., 1974).

Purcell, Edward L. and David F. Burg, eds., *The World Almanac of the American Revolution* (New York: World Almanac, 1992).

Document 5: Thompson, Benjamin. Reprinted in Henry Steele Commager and Richard B. Morris, eds., *The Spirit of Seventy-Six: The Story of the American Revolution as Told by its Participants* (New York: Harper and Row, 1975), 153–155.

Document 6: Paine, Thomas, *Common Sense*, 1776. Reprinted at "Milestone Historic Events." *Archiving Early America*, 2002. http://earlyamerica.com/earlyamerica/milestones/commonsense/text/html.

Document 7: Chalmers, James, *Plain Truth*, 1776. Reprinted by m. Christopher New, *Maryland, Loyalism and the American Revolution*, 1996. http://users.erols.com/candidus/plain-t.htm.

Document 8: U.S. Department of Commerce, Bureau of the Census, *Historical Statistics of the United States: Colonial Times to 1970* (Washington, D.C.: Government Printing Office, 1975), 1177.

Document 9: "Song of the Minuteman," 1777. Reprinted by Library of Congress, "America Singing: Nineteenth Century Song Sheets." *American Memory*, October 22, 1999. http://memory.loc.gov/ammem/amsshtml/amsshome.html.

Chapter 5: Political Parties and the New Nation

Document 1: Davidson, James West et al., *The American Nation* (Saddle River, N.Y.: Prentice Hall, 2000), 256.

Document 2: Alexander Hamilton to Edward Carrington, May 26, 1792. In "Primary Source Documents." *McGraw Hill Online Learning Center,* 2002. http://highered.mcgraw-hill.com/sites/0072417722/student_view0/chapter8/primary_source_documents.html.

Document 3: Thomas Jefferson to Thomas Pinckney, May 29, 1797. Reprinted in Merrill D. Patterson, ed., *Thomas Jefferson: Writings* (New York: Library of America 1984), 1045.

Document 4: Graebner, William and Leonard Richard, eds., *The American Record: Images of the Nation's Past* (New York: Knopf, 1982), 252 fig.

Document 5: "An Act, in Addition to the Act, Entitled 'An Act for the Punishment of Certain Crimes Against the United States.'" *The Avalon Project at the Yale Law School*, March 26, 2002. http://www.yale.edu/lawweb/avalon/statutes/sedact.htm.

Document 6: Fleming, Thomas, *Duel: Alexander Hamilton, Aaron Burr, and the Future of America* (New York: Basic Books, 1999), fig11a.

Document 7: "To All the Electors of Massachusetts . . ." March 28, 1808. Reprinted by Library of Congress, "An American Time Capsule: Three Centuries of Broadsides and Other Printed Ephemera." *American Memory*, November 30, 2000. http://memory.loc.gov/ammem/rbehtml/pehome.html.

Document 8: "The Gerrymander" 1812, ibid.

Chapter 6: Differences Between the North and the South

Document 1: U.S. Department of Commerce, *Historical Statistics,* 1172.

Document 2: Thomas Jefferson to John Adams, January 21, 1812. Reprinted in Merrill D. Patterson, ed., *Thomas Jefferson: Writings* (New York: The Library of America, 1984), 1259.

Document 3: Tocqueville, Alexis de, *Democracy in America*, trans. George Lawrence, ed. J. P. Mayer. (New York: Harper and Row, 1969), 245–248.

Document 4: Pratt, John Lowell, *Currier and Ives: Chronicles of America* (New York: Hammond, Inc. 1968), 191 fig.

Document 5: Mills, Henry A., "We are Destined to be a Great Manufacturing People." Reprinted in Erik Brun and Jay Crosby, eds., *Our Nation's Archive* (New York: Black Dog and Levanthal, 1999), 277–278.

Document 6: "Soho Saw and Planing Mill, Pittsburgh, PA." Library of Congress, Prints and Photographs Division, LC-USZ62-31978.

Document 7: Hayne, Robert Young, "Speech Before the United States Senate on Mr. Foote's Resolution" January 21, 1830. Reprinted in Lindsay Swift, ed., *The Great Debate Between Robert Young Hayne of South Carolina and Daniel Webster of Massachusetts.* (Boston: Houghton Mifflin 1898), 89, 100.

Document 8: Webster, Daniel, "Reply to Hayne" January 26 and 27, 1830. Reprinted in Swift, *The Great Debate*, 1898, 212–215.

Document 9: MacDonald, William ed., *Documentary Source Book of American History: 1606–1926* (New York: The MacMillan Co., 1937), 330–331.

Chapter 7: Slavery in the United States

Document 1: Douglass, Frederick, "Lecture on Slavery No. 1" December 1, 1850. Reprinted in Morton J. Frisch and Richard G. Stevens, eds., *Political Thought of American Statesmen* (Itasca, IL: F. E. Peacock Publishers Inc., 1973), 223.

Document 2: "GLC 227 Broadside: Great Sale of Land, Negroes, Corn and Other Property [slave sale] 24 November 1860." The Gilder Lehrman Collection, Courtesy of the Gilder Lehrman Institute of American History, New York.

Document 3: "Petition for Slavery in Georgia" December 9, 1738. Excerpted in William Dudley ed., *Slavery: Opposing Viewpoints* (San Diego, Calif.: Greenhaven Press Inc., 1992), 37, 38–39.

Document 4: Equiano, Olaudah, *The Interesting Narrative and Other Writings*, ed. Vincent Carretta (New York: Penguin Books, 1995), 56–59.

Document 5: Smith, Carter ed., *American Historical Images on File: The Black Experience* (New York: Facts on File, 1990), 1.10 fig.

Document 6: McDuffie, George, "Slavery is Just" 1835. In Dudley, *Slavery*, 66–67.

Document 7: Blasingame, John W., *The Slave Community: Plantation Life in the Antebellum South* (New York: Oxford University Press, 1972), 175, 361 (table 17).

Document 8: United States War Department, "Overseer Artayou Carrier Whipped Me . . . ," April 2, 1863. Still Picture Branch, National Archives and Records Administration, NWDNS-165-JT-230.

Document 9: Northup, Solomon, *Twelve Years a Slave*, 1853. Reprinted in Gilbert Osofsky ed., *Puttin on Ole Massa: Slave Narratives of Henry Bibb, William Wells Brown, and Solomon Northup* (New York: Harper and Row, 1969), 264–265.

Chapter 8: Reconstruction

Document 1: Alexander W. Matheson interview by Works Progress Administration, Federal Writers' Project. Reprinted by Library of Congress, "Manuscripts from the Federal Writers' Project 1936–1940." *American Memory*, October 19, 1998. http://memory.oc.gov/ammem/wpaintro/wpa.home.html.

Document 2: Wales, James Albert, "Everything Points to a Democratic Victory this Fall," *Harper's Weekly*, vol.18, no. 931, October 31, 1874, 901, fig.

Document 3: Bruce, Henry Clay, *The New Man: Twenty-Nine Years a Slave, Twenty-Nine Years a Free Man*. Electronic Edition encoded by Don Sechler and Natalia Smith, Academic Affairs Library University of North Carolina at Chapel Hill, 1997. http://docsouth.unc.edu/bruce/bruce.html, 112–118.

Document 4: Smith, *American Historical Images*, 1990, 3.25 fig.

Document 5: Nast, Thomas, "Worse than Slavery." *Harper's Weekly*, vol. 18, no. 930, October 24, 1874, 878.

Document 6: Edward W. Riley interviewed by Sheldon F. Gauthier, Federal Writers' Project, *American Memory*.

Document 7: Smith, *American Historical Images*, 1990, 3.10 fig.

Document 8: Warner, Charles Dudley, "The South Revisited" *Harper's Monthly Magazine*, March 1887, 638–639. Reprinted at "The Industrial Age," *The Gary Rutledge Learning Site*. http://garyrutledge.com/AmHistory/hist_articles/industrial_articles.htm.

Chapter 9: Immigration

Document 1: Nichols, Thomas L., "Lecture on Immigration and the Right of Naturalization," 1845. Excerpted in Tamara Roleff, ed., *Immigration: Opposing Viewpoints* (San Diego, Calif.: Greenhaven Press Inc., 1998), 20–21.

Document 2: Davis, Garrett, excerpted in Roleff, *Immigration,* 1998, 29–31.

Document 3: Hart, Alfred, "Chinese Working on Humboldt Plains," 1868. Reprinted at "History and Photos." *Union Pacific: Building America.* http://www.uprr.com/aboutup/photos/southernpacific/hart317.shtml.

Document 4: Conygnham, David Power, *The Irish Brigade and its Campaigns* (New York: Fordham University Press, 1994), 5–6.

Document 5: Claghorn, Kate Holladay, "Our Immigrants and Ourselves," *Atlantic Monthly*, vol. 86, issue 516, October 1900, 535–548. Reprinted by Library of Congress, "Nineteenth Century in Print: The Making of America in Books and Periodicals." *American Memory*, May 17, 2002. http://memory.loc.gov/ammem/ndlpcoop/moahtml/snchome.html.

Document 6: Keppler, Joseph, "Looking Backward," *Puck*, January 11, 1893. Republished by Roland Marchand, "Roland Marchand's Slide Collection." *History Project at U.C. Davis.Edu: A California History Social Science Project.* http://historyproject.ucdavis.edu/imageapplication/images.cfm?Major=IM&minor=F. Slide IM-F-39.

Document 7: Warne, Frank Julian, *The Immigrant Invasion.* Excerpted in Roleff, *Immigration*, 1998, 33–34.

Document 8: Coon, Peter Morton, *Ellis Island Interviews: In Their Own Words* (New York: Facts on File, 1997).

Novotny, Ann, *Strangers at the Door: Ellis Island, Castle Garden and the Great Migration to America* (Riverside, Conn.: The Chatham Press, Inc., 1971).

Document 9: Roskolenko, Harry, "America, the Thief." *The Time that Was Then.* (New York: Dial Press, 1971). Reprinted in Thomas C. Wheeler, ed., *The Immigrant Experience: The Anguish of Becoming American* (New York: Penguin Books, 1971), 154–155.

Chapter 10: The Growth of Industry

Document 1: Carnegie, Andrew, "Wealth," *North American Review*, vol. 148, issue 391, June 1889, 653–665. Reprinted by Library of Congress "Nineteenth Century in Print." *American Memory*, May 17, 2002.

Document 2: George, Henry, *Social Problems*, New York: 1883. Excerpted in William Dudley ed., *The Industrial Revolution: Opposing Viewpoints* (San Diego, Calif.: Greenhaven Press Inc. 1998), 71, 73.

Document 3: U.S. Department of Commerce, *Historical Statistics*, 1975, 176.

Document 4: Garland, Hamlin, "Homestead and Its Perilous Trades: Impressions of a Visit," *McClure's Magazine*, vol. III, June 1894, no.1. Reprinted by Patrick J. Hall, "Special World Wide Web Projects: American History," *The Ohio State University Department of History.* http://history.ohio-state.edu/projects/steel/june1894-garland_homestead.html.

Document 5: U.S. Department of Commerce and Labor, Children's Bureau, "Bibb Mill No. 1, Macon, Georgia . . ." by Lewis W. Hine, January 19, 1909. Still Pictures Branch, National Archives and Records Administration, NWDNS-102-LH-488.

Document 6: Harper, Ida Husted, "Women at Work," *Independent*, May 16, 1901. Excerpted in Dudley, *The Industrial Revolution* 1988, 198.

Document 7: Rockefeller, John D. *Random Reminiscences of Men and Events* (New York: Doubleday Page and Co. 1909), 57–59.

Document 8: Crane, Stephen, "In the Depths of a Coal Mine," *McClure's Magazine*, vol. III, August 1894, no. 3. Reprinted by Patrick J. Hall, "Special World Wide Web Projects: American History," *Ohio State University Department of History.* http://history.ohio-state.edu/projects/coal/CraneDepths/CraneDepths.htm.

Document 9: U.S. Department of Commerce, *Historical Statistics,* 1975, 693.

Chapter 11: The Progressive Era

Document 1: Tarbell, Ida, *The History of the Standard Oil Company,* 1904. Excerpted in "Clash of the Titans: Rockefeller vs. Tarbell," *American Experience: The Rockefellers* 1999–2000. http://www.pbs.org/wgbh/amex/rockefellers/sfeature/sf_6.html.

Document 2: Sinclair, Upton, *The Jungle,* 1906. Excerpted in Carl Jenson, *Stories that Changed America: Muckrakers of the 20th Century* (New York: Seven Stories Press 2000), 62.

Document 3: Roosevelt, Theodore, "Annual Message to Congress," December 5, 1905. HTML version by Gehrhard Peters, "Annual Messages to Congress on the State of the Union 1790–2002." *The American Presidency Project, University of California, Santa Barbara,* 1999–2002. http://www.presidency.ucsb.edu/docs/sou/rooseveltt5.htm.

Document 4: Diner, Steven J., *A Very Different Age: Americans of the Progressive Era* (New York: Hill and Wang, 1998).

Patterson, James T., *America in the Twentieth Century: A History* (New York: Harcourt Brace Jovanovich College Publishers 1989).

Document 5: *New York Times,* May 16, 1911, p.1.

New York Times, May 30, 1911, p. 1.

Document 6: U.S. Food and Drug Administration, "Federal Meat Inspection Act." *Laws Enforced by the FDA and Related Statutes,* September 11, 2002. http://www.fda.gov/opacom/laws/meat.htm.

Document 7: U.S. Constitution, Amendment 16.

U.S. Constitution, Amendment 17.

Document 8: "Calm About It . . ." Library of Congress, "By Popular Demand, Votes for Women: Suffrage Pictures 1850–1920." *American Memory,* October 19, 1998. http://memory.loc.gov/ammem/vfwhtml/vfwhome.html.

Chapter 12: America in the 1920s

Document 1: Held, John J. *Life,* February 18, 1926.

Document 2: Hughes, Langston, *Selected Poems of Langston Hughes* (New York: Knopf, 1959), 275.

(*The Collected Poems of Langston Hughes* by Langston Hughes copyright 1994 by the Estate of Langston Hughes. Used with permission of Alfred A. Knopf, a division of Random House, Inc.)

Document 3: Vanzetti, Bartolomeo, "Last Statement in Court." Quoted in Bruun and Crosby, *Nation's Archive,* 1999, 573.

Document 4: Stayton, William H., Congressional Digest, vol. 5, no.6, June 1926. Quoted in William Dudley, ed., *Opposing Viewpoints in American History Vol. II* (San Diego, Calif.: Greenhaven Press, Inc., 1996), 194–195.

Document 5: Rhodes, Harry Mellon, "Swimming," 1920. Library of Congress, "History of The American West, 1860–1920: Photographs from the Collections of the Denver Public Library." *American Memory,* July 25, 2000. http://memory.loc.gov/ammem/award97/codhtml/hawphome.html.

Document 6: "Ku Klux Klan Declaration" 1922. Quoted in Bruun and Crosby, *Nation's Archive*, 1999, 561.

Document 7: Smith, Alfred E., *Up to Now: An Autobiography* (New York: Viking Press 1929), 366–367.

Document 8: *New York Times*, November 23, 1922, p. 19.

Document 9: U.S. Department of Commerce, *Historical Statistics*, 1975, 716, 796.

Chapter 13: The New Deal

Document 1: Feldmeth, Greg D., "New Deal Programs," *U.S. History Resources*, March 31, 1998. http://home.earthlink.net/~gfeldmeth/chart.newdeal.html.

Hanson, David C., "New Deal Alphabet Agencies," *HIS122 Research Brief* 1999. http://www.vw.vccs.edu/vwhansd/His122/newdeal.html.

Document 2: Terkel, Studs, *Hard Times* (New York: Washington Square Press/Pocket Books 1970), 287

Document 3: Alice Timoney to President F. D. Roosevelt, FDR Library, Hyde Park, NY.

Document 4: "Civilian Conservation Corps Enrollees . . ." 1933. FDR Library, NLR-PHOCO-A-71146

Document 5: George E. Bigge interviewed by Abe Bortz, February 25, 1966. Social Security Administration "Oral History Interview," *Social Security Online History Page.* http://www.ssa.gov/history/biggeoral.html.

Document 6: Terkel, *Hard Times,* 316.

Document 7: U.S. Department of Commerce, *Historical Statistics,* 126.

Document 8: Terkel, *Hard Times*, 487.

Chapter 14: America in World War II

Document 1: Roosevelt, Franklin D., "State of the Union Address," January 6, 1942. Reprinted by Gehrhard Peters, *American Presidency Project.* http://presidency.ucsb.edu/site/docset/frameset_sou.htm.

Document 2: United States Office of War Information, "Production. Lockheed P-38 Pursuit Planes . . . ," July 1942. Library of Congress, "America from the Great Depression to World War II: Black and White Photographs from the FSA- OWI, 1935–1945." *American Memory,* December 15, 1998. http://memory.loc.gov/ammem/fsowhome.html

Document 3: United States Information Service Office of Government Reports, "Half the Metal in Every Ship . . ." Still Picture Branch, National Archives and Records Administration, NWDNS-44-PA-927.

Document 4: "Preliminary Agreement Between the United States and the United Kingdom," February 23, 1942. *The Avalon Project at the Yale Law School.* http://www.yale.edu/lawweb/avalon/decade/decade04.htm.

Document 5: Dear, I.C.B. ed., "Statistics" *The Oxford Companion to World War II* (New York: Oxford University Press 1995), 1060.

Document 6: United States Office for Emergency Management War Production Board, "Give Us More of These," 1942–1943. Still Picture Branch National Archives, NWDNS-179-WP-230.

Document 7: Gregory, Ross, *Almanacs of American Life: Modern America 1914–1945* (New York: Facts on File, 1995), 251.

Document 8: United States Office of War Information, Overseas Picture Division, "If It'll Save a Second . . . ," 1944. Library of Congress, "America from the Great Depression." *American Memory.*

Document 9: Gregory, *Almanacs*, 246.

Chapter 15: America and the Cold War

Document 1: Kennan, George, "Excerpts from Telegraphic Message from Moscow," February 22, 1946. Reprinted in "Documents Relating to American Foreign Policy," *Mount Holyoke Department of International Relations*, January 13, 2001. http://www.mtholyoke.edu/acad/intrel/longtel.html.

Document 2: U.S. Federal Emergency Management Agency, "Temporary Basement Fallout Shelter," 1957. Still Picture Branch National Archives, NWDNS-311-D-14(1).

Document 3: National Security Council, "Discussion at the 339th Meeting of the National Security Council," Thursday, October 10, 1957. Roger D. Laurius, NASA chief historian, "Sputnik, The Fortieth Anniversary." *The NASA History Homepage*, October 16, 2000. http://hq.nasa.gov/office/pao/history/sputnik/oct57.html.

Document 4: U.S. Department of Defense United States Marine Corps, "Atomic Energy Commission Proving Grounds, Nevada . . . ," May 1, 1952. Still Picture Branch, National Archives, NWDNS-127-N-A325011.

Document 5: Lawson, Jon Howard, "Statement to the House Un-American Activities Committee." Reprinted in Eric Bently, ed., *Thirty Years of Treason* (New York: Viking Press, 1971), 161–163.

Document 6: U.S. Central Intelligence Agency, "Gary Powers (Soviets Broadcast Powers Trial)," August 17, 1960. *Freedom of Information Act Electronic Reading Room.* http://www.foia.cia.gov/.

Document 7: "Duck and Cover Drills," *The Detroit News: Rear View Mirror.* http://detnews.com/history/shelters/shelters.htm.

Document 8: Kennedy, John F., "Address on the Cuban Missile Crisis," October 22, 1962. Reprinted at "American Source Documents: the Sixties," *History Central.* http://www.multied.com/jfkcuba.txt.

Document 9: Natural Resources Defense Council, "Table of U.S. Nuclear Warheads 1945–1970/1971–1996." http://www.nrdc.org/nuclear/nudb/datab9.asp.

———."Table of USSR/Russian Nuclear Warheads, 1949–1970/1971–1996." http://www.nrdc.org/nuclear/nudb/datab10.asp.

Chapter 16: The Civil Rights Movement

Document 1: United States Information Agency, "Civil Rights March on Washington, D.C. [Leaders Marching Down the Street], August 28, 1963. Still Picture Branch, National Archives, NWDNS-306SSM-4C(35)6.

Document 2: King, Martin Luther, "I Have a Dream," August 28, 1963. Reprinted by *The Avalon Project at Yale Law School.* http://www.yale.edu/law/lawweb/avalon/treatise/king/mlk01.htm.

Document 3: Antell, Gerson, Walter Harris and William S. Dobkin, *Current Issues in American Democracy* (New York: Amsco School Publications 1992).

Winters, Paul A., *The Civil Rights Movement: Turning Points in World History* (San Diego, Calif.: Greenhaven Press Inc. 2000).

Document 4: Patterson, *America in the Twentieth Century,* 390.

Document 5: Johnson, Lyndon B., "Executive Order No. 11246," September 28, 1965. U.S. "Laws Enforced by the Equal Employment Opportunity Commission," January 15, 1997. http://www.eeoc.gov/35th/thelaw/eo-11246.html.

Document 6: Ellison, Phyllis quoted in Harry Hampton and Steve Fayer, *Voices of Freedom: An Oral History of the Civil Rights Movement from the 1950s Through the 1980s* (New York: Bantam Books 1990), 600–601.

Document 7: Cose, Ellis, *The Rage of a Privileged Class,* excerpted in Paul A. Winters, ed., *Race Relations: Opposing Viewpoints* (San Diego, Calif.: Greenhaven Press Inc. 1996), 98–99.

SOURCES FOR WORKS CITED

Document 8: U.S. Department of Commerce Bureau of the Census, *Historical Income Tables—People*, "Full Time, Year Round, Black Workers by Mean Income and Sex 1955–2000," table P-37b. http://www.census.gov/hhes/income/histinc/p37bx1.html.

———, *Historical Income Tables—People*, "Full Time, Year Round, White Workers by Mean Income and Sex 1955–2000," Table P-37a. http://www.census.gov/hhes/income/histinc/p37ax1.html.

Document 9: Campbell, Clarice T. *Civil Rights Chronicle: Letters from the South.* (Jackson, Miss.: Univ. Press of Mississippi, 1997), xiii.

COPYRIGHT ACKNOWLEDGMENTS

The author and publisher wish to thank those who have generously given permission to reprint borrowed material:

Excerpts from *Notes Among the Indians* by Vincent Colyer (page 5) and *Indian Boyhood* by Charles Alexander Eastman (page 7) are reprinted by permission of the Rector and Visitors of the University of Virginia and the Electronic Text Center http://etext.lib.virginia.edu.

The photograph "Snaketown Canal #409" (page 3) is used by permission of Arizona State Museum, University of Arizona.

"The Caravel" (page 11) from *The Voyage of Verrazano* by Henry C. Murphy. Published by J. Munsell, 1875. Used courtesy of the New York Public Library, Print Collection.

Photograph of astrolabe (page 13) is used courtesy of Adler Planetarium & Astronomy Museum, Chicago, Illinois

Excerpt from "A Discourse on Western Planting" by Richard A. Hakluyt (page 16) is reprinted by permission from *The Collections of the Maine Historical Society* (1831-1906), Series 2, Volume 2.

"The Bloody Massacre" by Paul Revere (page 28) is used courtesy of The American Antiquarian Society. Copyright © The American Antiquarian Society.

" 'Republicans Turn Out, Turn Out...' Jefferson and Clinton Campaign Poster," (page 41) 1804, negative number 35609, from the Collection of the New-York Historical Society. Courtesy of The New-York Historical Society.

"Death of Alexander Hamilton" (page 43) is used courtesy of the New York Public Library, Print Collection.

"Broadside: Great Sale of Land, Negroes, Corn & Other Property," (page 60) November 24, 1860, from The Gilder Lehrman Collection, GLC 227. Courtesy of the Gilder Lehrman Institute of American History, New York.

"Looking Backward" (page 85) by Joseph Keppler from *Puck*, January 11, 1893. Courtesy of the New York Public Library, Print Collection.

"I, Too, Sign America" (page 110) from *The Collected Poems of Langston Hughes* by Langston Hughes. Copyright © 1994 by The Estate of Langston Hughes. Used by permission of Alfred A. Knopf, a division of Random House, Inc.

Photograph of "Duck and Cover Drill" (page 147) from the Detroit News Archives. Reprinted by permission of the Detroit News.

INDEX

Affirmative Action, 156
American Revolution, 27–36
Astrolabe, 13
Aztecs, 12

Beijing, 10
Boston Massacre, 28
Britain: losses in World War II, 138; strength in
    Revolutionary War, 31; value of U.S. trade with,
    34
Busing, 157

Caravel, 11
Carnegie, Andrew, 91
Chalmers, James, 33
Cheyenne, 6
Chinese Immigrants, 82
Civil Rights Movement, 151–160
Cold War, 140–150
Colonial America, 19–26
Columbian Exchange, 17
Common Sense, 33
Connecticut, 22
Continental Army, 31, 32
Conyngham, David P., 83
Cortes, Hernan, 12
Cuban Missile Crisis, 148

Davis, Garrett, 81
Declaration of the Causes and Necessity of Taking
    Up Arms, 30
Democracy in America, 50
Democratic-Republicans, 38; election advertisement,
    41
Douglass, Frederick, 59

Exploration, Age of, 9–18

Federalists, 38; accused of loyalty to Britain, 40
Freedmen, 72; schools for, 76

German Immigrants, 81, 84
Gerrymander, *cartoon*, 45
Great Depression, unemployment during, 126

Hakluyt, Richard, 16
Hamilton, Alexander: criticizes Jefferson, 39;
    differences with Jefferson, 38; death of, 43
Hayne, Robert Young, 54
Hohokum, 3
Homestead, PA, description of, 93
Hopi, 2
House of Burgesses, 25
House Un-American Activities Committee (HUAC),
    145
Hughes, Langston, *I, Too, Sing America*, 110
Hulton, Anne, 29

Immigration, 79–89. *See also specific groups*
Industry, growth of, 90–98
Inuit, 2
Irish immigrants, 83
Iroquois, 2

Jefferson, Thomas: criticized by Hamilton, 39;
    differences with Hamilton, 38; letter to Adams,
    49; on origin of parties, 40
Jewish immigrants, 88

Kennan, George F., 141
Kennedy, John F., and Cuban Missle Crisis, 148
King, Dr. Martin Luther, 152; *I Have a Dream*, 153

Labor Unions, rise of, 92
Las Casas, Bartolome de, 14

Lend Lease Agreement, 133
Lowell, MA, description of, 54

Manufacturing: cotton mill, 94; in Homestead, PA, 93; in Lowell, MA, 52; in Pittsburgh, PA, 53; steel production, 97
Maryland, 20
McDuffie, George, 64
Meat Inspection Act, 104
Minute Man, 35
Mississippi, cotton plantation, 51

Native Americans, 1–8. *See also specific groups*
New Deal, 119–128. *See also* Great Depression
Nichols, Thomas L., 80
Nullification, Ordinance of, 56

Paine, Thomas, 33
Pittsburgh, PA, 53
Political Parties, development of, 37–46
Polo, Marco, 10
Progressive Era, 99–107
Prohibition, criticism of, 112

Reconstruction, 69–78
Revere, Paul, 28
Rockerfeller, John D., 96
Roosevelt, Franklin D., 122, 130
Roosevelt, Theodore, 101

Sedition Act, 42
Sinclair, Upton, *The Jungle*, 101

Sioux, 2
Slave Factory, 15
Slavery, Slaves, 58–68; among Native Americans, 14; auction, 60, 67; colonial imports of, 48; effect on the South, 50; mistreatment of, 63, 66; slave factory, 15; slave ship, 24, 62
Smith, Al, 115
Soviet Union: cold war assessment of, 141; nuclear arsenal of, 149; report on U-2 incident, 146; World War II, losses of, 138
Sputnik, U.S. reaction to, 143
Standard Oil Co., 96; *History of the Standard Oil Co.*, 100; dissolved, 103

Tipi, 6
Tocqueville, Alexis de, 50
Toleration, Act of, 20
Travois, 6

United States: colonial trade of, 34; nuclear arsenal of, 149; power in Revolutionary War, 31; steel production of, 97; World War II production of, 134

Vanzetti, Bartolomeo, 111
Voting, Qualifications for, 21
Voting Rights Act, effects of, 155

Webster, Daniel, 55
Witchitas, 5
Women: at work, 95; colonial rights of, 23; suffrage, 106
World War II, 129–139; casualties, costs of, 138

ABOUT THE AUTHOR

EDWARD O'CONNOR has been teaching social studies in New York State for 15 years. A first time author, he lives with his wife and two children in the Hudson Valley.

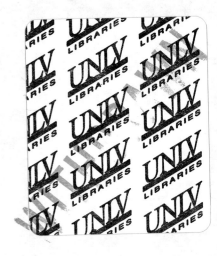